FREUD ON RITUAL
Reconstruction and Critique

American Academy of Religion Dissertation Series

edited by
H. Ganse Little, Jr.

Number 26

FREUD ON RITUAL
Reconstruction and Critique
by
Volney P. Gay

Volney Patrick Gay

FREUD ON RITUAL
Reconstruction
and Critique

Scholars Press

Distributed by
Scholars Press
PO Box 5207
Missoula, Montana 59806

FREUD ON RITUAL
Reconstruction and Critique

Volney P. Gay
Department of Religious Studies, McMaster University
Hamilton, Ontario

Ph.D., 1976
University of Chicago

Adviser:
Don S. Browning

Library of Congress Cataloging in Publication Data

Gay, Volney Patrick.
   Freud on ritual.

   (Dissertation series - American Academy of Religion ;
26 ISSN 0145-272X)
   Originally presented as the author's thesis, University
of Chicago, 1976.
   Bibliography: p.
   1. Ritual. 2. Freud, Sigmund, 1856-1939. I. Title.
II. Series: American Academy of Religion. Dissertation
series - American Academy of Religion ; 26.
BL600.G36   1979   200'.1'9   79-11385
ISBN 0-89130-282-4
ISBN 0-89130-301-4 pbk.

Printed in the United States of America
1   2   3   4   5
Edwards Brothers, Inc.
Ann Arbor, MI 48104

To the Memory of
W. B. Blakemore, Dean
Disciples Divinity House
University of Chicago

TABLE OF CONTENTS

ACKNOWLEDGEMENTS

Nietzsche says somewhere that if authors were more honest they would cease speaking of 'my book' and instead refer to 'our book'. This is especially true of dissertation writers whose modest crafts are often made of timbers hewn, shaped, and placed by previous hands. It was Freud's singular privilege to be the Darwin of Psychology. It was my privilege to read him and construct this essay with the help of Professors Don S. Browning, Peter Homans, and Paul Ricoeur, all of the University of Chicago. I thank them for their instruction and encouragement.

I also thank Barbara Gay, Helen Bailey, Carmella Marasco, and John and Andrea Briggs for their aid in the preparation of this manuscript.

Finally I would like to thank Dr. R. C. McIvor, Dean of Social Sciences, McMaster University. His prompt financial support expedited the appearance of this monograph.

V. P. G.

CHAPTER I

INTRODUCTION: RHETORIC VERSUS METAPSYCHOLOGY

Among the many available discussions of Freud's psychology
of religion one can find critical analyses of the cultural assumptions upon which he mounted his attacks on religion,[1] of
his particular application of psychoanalytic theory to religious
experience,[2] and of the pseudoenergetics that dominate his writings and so obscure the actual (philosophic) hermeneutic which
underlies them.[3]

While these studies have added to our understanding of
Freud's texts, there is one aspect of his earliest works on
religion in respect to which they require supplement. Each of
these authors appears to accept the claim that in his earliest
published remarks on religion and psychopathology,[4] Freud established or thought he established that the psychological
mechanism responsible for the formation of obsessional-neurotic
behavior was also responsible for the formation of apparently
normal religious ritual acts. Their acceptance of this claim
is understandable since Freud makes it abundantly clear that he
himself believes ritual actions and obsessive behavior are essentially similar phenomena; "...one might describe neurosis as
individual religiosity and religion as a universal neurosis."[5]

Although one might argue that similar phenomena are not
necessarily identical to one another, it is clear from this
essay and his later works on religious thought and institutions
that Freud very much believes that certain similarities which
religious rituals bear to (neurotic) obsessive actions such as
prayers, invocations, acts of contrition, etc., are manifestations
of the workings of the same psychological mechanism: repression.
Both orthodox and nonorthodox psychoanalysts support this reading of Freud's argument. In his description of the composition
of the 1907 essay, Ernest Jones, Freud's chief biographer, summarizes its conclusions in a way that clearly indicates he believes Freud uncovered the repressive origins of religious
ritual: "In obsessional neurosis the repressed impulses that
have to be kept at bay are typically sexual ones; in religion

1

they may also be so, but more characteristically are selfish or
aggressive (anti-social) ones."[6] A. Bronson Feldman says of
the 1907 paper:

> The core of the essay consists of proof that the mode
> of combatting sexual impulses in the case of obses-
> sional neurosis and the mode of combatting tendencies
> outlawed by holy impulse were the same for both sick-
> ness and sanctity.[7]

It is my thesis that, in opposition to his rhetorical expressions and to the usual acceptance of their psychoanalytic
validity, Freud never demonstrated and in fact never claimed
(in the 1907 essay) that religious rituals shared with obsessive actions a common genesis in the workings of repression.
On the contrary, I argue that the actual theoretic propositions
Freud uses in the essay suggest that ritual behavior is a product of the nonpathological, often beneficial, mechanism of
suppression. If my argument is sound, it follows that we must
reexamine Freud's later writings on religion and ritual which
appeal to the theoretic validity of this earliest essay and we
must, once more, attempt to account for the observable benefits
that many practitioners of ritual enjoy.

The Importance of the 1907 Essay for
Freud's Analysis of Religion

The significance of my thesis is a function of the significance of the 1907 essay in relation to the entire psychoanalytic corpus on religious behavior. I should like to argue that
the essay represents the bedrock upon which Freud erected many
of his later theories of religious thought and behavior. My
reasons for saying this are threefold.

(1) Speaking within an analytic mode, the essay expresses
thoughts and feelings about religion which, according to Jones,[8]
dominated Freud's earliest experiences and which therefore may
be considered to be genetically primary events. It then follows, speaking from the genetic point of view, that these formulations will be both archetypical of later discoveries by the
same author and will tend to exercise a major (retrogressive)
influence upon his later formulations and analyses of the same
phenomenon. We can see this in Freud's later writings on

religion and ritual in which he says that the beneficial effects rituals have upon many persons are due to their essentially pathological genesis in the function of repression. This
is a tidy formulation which, while recognizing the emotional
benefits rituals offer to many, criticizes them by explaining
that they are effective just because they employ the (pathological) mechanism (repression) which, when operant in the individual, creates the particular deviancies of the lonely neurotic.

For example, in his essay on Leonardo, Freud explained the
relevance of the oedipal complex to both public religious behavior and to private obsessions.

> The protection against neurotic illness, which reli-
> gion vouchsafes to those who believe in it, is easily
> explained: it removes their parental [oedipal] com-
> plex, on which the sense of guilt in individuals as
> well as in the whole human race depends, and disposes
> of it, while the unbeliever has to grapple with the
> problem on his own.[9]

A few years later, Freud reenforced this claim when he
suggested that *individual* neuroses are functional equivalents
of public (cultural) institutions, such as religion and morality: "...the neuroses themselves have turned out to be attempts
to find individual solutions to the problems of compensating
unsatisfied wishes, while the institutions seek to provide
social solutions for these same problems."[10]

He repeats and enlarges this claim in his preface to T.
Reik's study on ritual.[11]

> It is impossible to escape the conclusion that these
> [psychoanalytic] patients are, in an *asocial* fashion,
> making the very attempts at solving their conflicts and
> appeasing their pressing needs which, when those at-
> tempts are carried out in a fashion that is acceptable
> to the majority, are known as poetry, religion, and
> philosophy.[12]

He states this theme even more polemically and curtly in
The Future of an Illusion.

> ...devout believers are safeguarded in a high degree
> against the risk of certain neurotic illnesses; their
> acceptance of the universal neurosis spares them the
> task of constructing a personal one.[13]

(2) The 1907 essay occupies a seemingly unassailable place both within psychoanalytic and nonanalytic assessments of Freud's psychology of religion. While Reiff, Fromm, and Ricoeur as well as others who are intimately familiar with psychoanalytic theory allude to the importance of the 1907 essay, none of them directly examines the validity of its theoretic arguments. Others, such as Philip,[14] who write from a theological orientation and who criticize Freud's generalizations about religion, seem to regard the claims Freud makes about the repressive nature of ritual as clinical observations or scientific verities and therefore not susceptible to textual or logical criticism.

(3) Finally, and most importantly, having postulated that the mechanism of repression secretly linked obsessional acts with religious practices, Freud found that he had created an exemplary model by which he could extend psychoanalytic principles of interpretation beyond the individual patient and his symptoms to the culture and its discontents.

By isolating the psychopathogenic mechanism of repression and declaring it to be an invariable constituent of all ritual behavior, Freud was able to traverse the logical space that had separated the analysis of dreams from the analysis of myths, the analysis of the individual from the analysis of his group, and the analysis of private, individual, symbols from the analysis of those which are universal. His theory of the psychopathology of ritual is an integral part of his attempt to establish psychoanalysis as a general psychology.[15] In the brilliant works of the first decade of this century, he applied the narrow methods and concepts which originated with his and Breurer's studies on hysteria to the study of dreams,[16] everyday mannerisms and character,[17] and developmental psychology.[18] In each of these works he employed the concept of repression which, by virtue of its embodiment of the distinction conscious-unconscious, offered a concise and nearly universal explanation of conflictual behavior and ambivalent feelings as they are expressed in the "normal" phenomena of jokes, slips of the pen, dreams, fantasies, and mannerisms.[19]

Repression, which may be defined as the process or mechanism by which an impulse or wish is denied access to consciousness, is a central concept in the psychoanalytic hermeneutic armamentarium. For example, if we view religious ritual as publicly validated obsessive behavior, it follows that we may examine the thinking processes and products called "theology" in the same way and with the same goals as when we analyze the rationalizations neurotics offer as explanations of their obsessive actions. In both cases we would expect to encounter more or less elaborate "stories" which, like other psychoneurotic symptoms, could be reduced, via analysis, to their essential elements: a dangerous wish originating in the id is covered over and yet expressed by a counter-effort originating in the ego.

Also, having "discovered" the existence of repression in the formation of religious ritual, artistic productions, and other nonclinical behaviors, Freud was able to reverse interpretative directions and claim that many of the themes and contents of these nonclinical phenomena illustrated the validity of psychoanalytic clinical interpretations.

> How do we profess to arrive at the meaning of these
> dream-symbols, about which the dreamer himself can
> give us little or no information. My answer is that
> we derive our knowledge from widely different sources:
> from fairy tales, and myths, jokes and witticisms,
> from folklore...and from poetic and colloquial usage
> of language.[20]

In summary, I am suggesting that the validity of the theoretic contentions (the metapsychology) of the 1907 essay is crucial both to our assessment of Freud's psychology of religion and of his psychoanalysis of culture.

Rhetoric Versus Metapsychology in the 1907 Essay

After a brief discussion of the mechanism of displacement which he says operates in both obsessional and religious acts, Freud summarizes the essay as follows.

> The most essential similarity [between obsessional
> and religious acts] would reside in the underlying
> renunciation of the activation of instincts that are

constitutionally present; and the chief difference
would lie in the nature of those instincts, which in
the neuroses are exclusively sexual in their origin,
while in religion they spring from egoistic sources.[21]

I have two criticisms of this last sentence. First, from the
economic point of view, it would seem that the chief experiential difference between neurotic and religious acts lies in the
quality and quantity of anxiety typical of each in that the
former are marked by an abundance of anxiety while the latter
are not.

Second, and more important to my thesis, an analysis of
Freud's technical description of the anti-instinctual processes
typical of both kinds of behavior reveals that he consistently
distinguished the mechanism of *repression* which he says operates in the formation of obsessional neurosis from that of
suppression or renunciation which he ascribes to religious
behavior.

An examination of certain key sentences in the essay may
make this clearer.

The primary fact which lies at the bottom of obsessional neurosis is always *"the repression of an instinctual impulse..."*[22]	= "Verdrängung einer Triebregung"[23]
"The formation of religion... seems to be based on the suppression, the renunciation of, certain instinctual impulses."[24]	= "...der Religionsbildung scheint die Unterdrückung, der Verzicht auf gewisse Triebregungen zugrunde zu liegen."[25]

Throughout most of the essay,[26] Freud carefully describes
the anti-instinctual mechanism typical of obsessive acts as
Verdrängung (repression) and that which is typical of religious
acts as *Unterdrückung* (suppression) or as *Verzicht* (renunciation). This linguistic distinction seems significant in light
of the crucial topographic and dynamic differences by which
Freud distinguished the two processes. Since even in the
earliest analytic literature "repression" was said to be one of
the main features in the genesis of neurotic disorders, and
since Freud's goal in this essay is to demonstrate an underlying similarity between obsessional acts and religious behavior,
we would expect him to demonstrate that repression is the

fundamental mechanism responsible for the formation of religious ceremonies. However, he does not.

The most essential similarity would reside in the underlying renunciation of the activation of instincts that are constitutionally present.[27]	Die wesentlichste Übereinstimmung läge in dem zugrunde liegenden Verzicht auf die Batätigung von konstitutionell gegebenen Trieben....[28]

It is clear from other passages in the essay that Freud meant to equate "renunciation" with "suppression" (to equate *Verzicht* with *Unterdrückung*). The nearly deliberative, fully conscious, and judgmental meaning of the former term is evident in its alternate English translation, "resignation." Clearly, one can only renounce a desire or resign from an attempt to fulfill it if one is fully conscious of entertaining it as a wish which is either to be granted in the future or fulfilled, through fantasy expression, in the present.

However, it is clear both from this essay and the later metapsychological essays, especially the essay on repression,[29] that repression involves essentially unconscious processes which are not available to deliberation or judgment; "...the essence of repression lies simply in turning something away, and keeping it at a distance, from the conscious."[30]

I am not arguing that renunciation (or suppression) is or is not fundamental to the elaboration of religious behavior. I am only pointing out that, according to Freud's own theoretic texts, suppression is not identical with the process of repression. This has two important consequences for Freud's attempt, in the 1907 essay, to identify religious acts with obsessive behavior. First, it offers prima facie evidence that the former sort of actions are in terms of Freud's own theory of neurotogenesis, essentially unlike the latter sort. Second, in terms of Freud's theory of anxiety, we are forced to distinguish anxiety which arises from the effects of repression from anxiety which arises from reality-based perceptions of potentially dangerous circumstances. In a number of works, including one written in the same year as the essay on religious acts,[31] Freud states that neurotic anxiety occurs as a result of the *repression* of instinctual impulses: "The anxiety in anxiety-dreams, like neurotic anxiety in general,...arises out of libido by the process of repression."[32]

If neurotic anxiety is a function of repression, and if the anti-instinctual mechanism typical of religious acts is suppression (and not repression), then it would seem to follow that the "anxiety" which Freud ascribes to pious individuals who perform certain religious rituals cannot be neurotic anxiety.

Of course the trust and hope which the pious place upon their ritual acts may be quite misbased in fact and have their origins in dynamically unconscious notions of grandiosity, the omnipotence of thoughts, and other fantasies typical of the neurotic. However, it is not a man's fantasies which make him a neurotic, it is his ego's response to those fantasies, namely repression, which determines the extent of the symptoms generated by internal conflict.

If we assume with Freud that the pious person's ego does not repress, but only suppresses, it follows that his worries and behavior cannot rightly be called neurotic.[33]

Summary

As noted above, many authors have explored the descriptive accuracy of Freud's views on religion. A few, such as Ricoeur,[34] have analyzed the philosophic validity of his application of clinically derived, psychoanalytic, theories to nonpathological, nonclinical, phenomena. In harmony with Ricoeur's aims, but in contrast to his method, I propose to examine and criticize Freud's metapsychological arguments themselves from both (1) Freud's own formulations, especially the papers on metapsychology, and (2) later additions to the analytic theory of ego defense and ego development.

My major concern is to examine Freud's claims concerning the repressive features of religious ritual in light of the metapsychological reasoning he employed. On the basis of close textual analysis, I argue that he failed to prove that religious rituals are essentially obsessivelike behavior. If I am correct, it then follows that we must, once more, attempt to explain the uncontested fact that some religious rituals are of obvious benefit to some people.

In this first chapter I reviewed the actual metapsychological arguments Freud used in his central texts on religion. In the second, my major goal is to show that he incorrectly used an originally weak clinical model of obsessional neurosis as a strong model to explain, and ultimately, condemn religious ritual.

Recognizing the limitations of that model, I propose, in Chapter III, to forge a neutral definition of ritual which does not beg the question of the psychopathological nature of that phenomenon. With that definition in hand, I suggest we can re-approach Freud's entire corpus looking for a text or texts which most directly reflect the dimensions of our neutral definition. I suggest that *Beyond the Pleasure Principle*,[35] written in 1920, fulfills that requirement. I analyze that text chapter by chapter drawing out what appear to be the central metapsychological concepts most directly relevant to the varieties of ritual action Freud discusses in it.

In the following chapters I review the way in which those metapsychological concepts developed over the course of Freud's career. In the last, Chapter VII, I suggest that contrary to his theological opinions, Freud's psychology of the ego entails the strong hypothesis that it develops through and encourages ritualized patterns of behavior.

Thus this work is a rereading and reflection upon core psychoanalytic theories about religious ritual in light of my claim that Freud never established that ritual actions were essentially functions of the pathogenic mechanism of repression. If I am correct, it follows that Freud and his followers misapplied the full-fledged metapsychology of psychoanalytic theory. And if this is correct, then this essay can serve as a prolegomenon to future attempts to raise those questions about the nature of religious ritual which Freud and others felt had been answered in the past.

Sections of this chapter are reprinted from *Psychoanalytic Review* 62/3 (1975) through the courtesy of the editors and the publisher, the National Psychological Association for Psychoanalysis, New York, New York.

NOTES

CHAPTER I

[1]Philip Rieff, *Freud: The Mind of the Moralist* (New York: Doubleday, 1959).

[2]Erich Fromm, *Psychoanalysis and Faith* (New Haven: Yale University, 1950).

[3]Paul Ricoeur, *Freud and Philosophy* (New Haven: Yale University, 1970).

[4]Unless otherwise noted, all references to Freud's writings are taken from *The Standard Edition of the Complete Psychological Works of Sigmund Freud* (24 vols.; trans. and ed. James Strachey; London: Hogart Press and the Institute of Psycho-Analysis, 1953-1974) (hereafter cited as *SE*). See Sigmund Freud, "Obsessive Actions and Religious Practices," *SE* 9 (1959 [1907b]) 116-127.

[5]Ibid., 126-127.

[6]Ernest Jones, *The Life and Work of Sigmund Freud* 2 (3 vols.; New York: Basic Books, 1953-1957) 339.

[7]A. Bronson Feldman, "Freudian Theology," *Psychoanalysis: Journal of Psychoanalytic Psychology* 1/3 (1953) 34.

[8]Jones, *Life and Work*, 19.

[9]Sigmund Freud, *Leonardo da Vinci and a Memory of His Childhood*, *SE* 11 (1957 [1910c]) 123.

[10]Idem, "The Claims of Psycho-Analysis to Scientific Interest," *SE* 13 (1953 [1913j]) 186.

[11]Theodor Reik, *Ritual: Psycho-Analytic Studies* (London: Hogarth Press, 1931).

[12]Sigmund Freud, "Preface to Reik's *Ritual: Psycho-Analytic Studies*," *SE* 17 (1955 [1919g]) 261.

[13]Idem, *The Future of an Illusion*, *SE* 21 (1961 [1927c]) 44.

[14]H. Philip, *Freud and Religious Belief* (London: Rockliff, 1956).

[15]Cf. Heinz Hartmann, *Ego Psychology and the Problem of Adaptation* (New York: International Universities Press, 1961 [1939]).

[16]Sigmund Freud, *The Interpretation of Dreams*, *SE* 4 and 5 (1953 [1900a]).

11

[17] Idem, *The Psychopathology of Everyday Life*, *SE* 6 (1960 [1901b]).

[18] Idem, *Three Essays on the Theory of Sexuality*, *SE* 7 (1953 [1905d]) 125-243.

[19] Psychoanalytic hermeneutics was and is essentially dialectic: manifest, conscious actions are opposed to latent, unconscious, desires (wishes); instinctual drive is opposed to psychological structure; the individual is opposed to the group; fantasy and the inner life is opposed to reality and the outer world. The structural point of view introduced in the twenties would seem to be nondialectical in that three intrapsychic structures (the ego, id, and superego) are granted a degree of functional independence. However, for Freud it is clear that the superego is genetically a part of the ego from which it derives its form and through which it functions. Also, we note that the dialectic spirit persisted in Freud's last works in which he formulated the grand dichotomies of life-instinct and death-instinct, of Eros and Thanatos.

[20] Sigmund Freud, *Introductory Lectures on Psycho-Analysis*, *SE* 15 and 16 (1961 and 1963 [1916-1917]) 158-159, slightly altered.

[21] Idem, "Obsessive Actions and Religious Practices," 124.

[22] Ibid.

[23] Sigmund Freud, *Gesammelte Schriften* 7 (12 vols.; Vienna: International Psychoanalytic Press, 1924-1934) 136 (hereafter cited as *GS*).

[24] Idem, "Obsessive Actions and Religious Practices," 125.

[25] Idem, *GS* 7.137.

[26] While Freud never associates *Verdrängung* with (normal) religious actions, he does, sometimes, say that obsessive actions may represent the workings of *Unterdrückung*, e.g., "Obsessive Actions and Religious Practices," 127. This suggests that he views "repression" as a particular type of "suppression."

[27] Ibid.

[28] Freud, *GS* 7.139.

[29] Idem, "Repression," *SE* 14 (1957 [1915d]) 143-158.

[30] Ibid., 147.

[31] Sigmund Freud, *Delusions and Dreams in Jensen's 'Gradiva'*, *SE* 9 (1959 [1907a]) 3-95.

[32] Ibid., 60-61.

[33] For a more detailed analysis of this essay, see my article, "Psychopathology and Ritual: Freud's Essay 'Obsessive Actions and Religious Practices,'" *Psychoanalytic Review* 62/3 (1975) 493-507.

[34] Ricoeur, *Freud and Philosophy*.

[35] Sigmund Freud, *Beyond the Pleasure Principle*, *SE* 18 (1955 [1920g]) 7-64.

CHAPTER II

THE MODEL OF OBSESSIONAL NEUROSIS IN THE
LATER TEXTS ON RELIGION

In this chapter I should like to examine the role Freud
assigned to the ritual-as-neurosis model in his later works on
religion. I shall contend that he gradually alters the actual
metapsychological arguments that initially distinguished religious ritual and neurotic actions in favor of the overt rhetoric
of the 1907 essay. In short, as we will see below, by the time
of the composition of *Moses and Monotheism*, around 1934, he
straightforwardly asserted that religious ritual made use of
precisely those repressive mechanisms that characterize neurotic behavior.

First I will discuss how I intend to use the often misused
term "model" in the succeeding chapters on the various models
of mental functioning which emerged in Freud's metapsychology.
Second, I briefly review the model of obsessional neurosis
which Freud elaborated upon in "Notes Upon a Case of Obsessional Neurosis" (the "Rat Man"). Third, I indicate the ways in
which Freud used that model in *Totem and Taboo* to explain religion in general and religious ritual in particular. In the
last part of this chapter I conclude that because the clinical
model of obsessional neurosis entails the repression hypothesis
and because, as we have seen, Freud never showed that religious
rituals exemplified repressive behaviors, it follows that when
he uses the model of obsessional neurosis to explain religious
behavior he does so on inadequate metapsychological grounds.

Models, Metaphors, and The Interpretation of Culture

Although one hears the term "model" used indiscriminately
in a variety of contexts, its proper home appears to be nearer
cybernetics and research on artificial intelligence than it
does psychoanalytic theory.[1]

Indeed, Freud was consistently more subtle than his co-
workers during the middle-phase of his work in that he always
avoided making the bald reductive assertion that religion is a

form of obsessional neurosis, based upon the repression of
instinct, *tout court*. Thus in his article for the magazine
Scientia, he summarizes the general psychoanalytic approach to
a variety of cultural phenomena, including religion, as one
which seeks to use "...the psycho-analytic mode of thought...
like a new instrument of research. The application of its
hypotheses to social psychology enables us both to raise fresh
problems and to see old ones in a fresh light and contribute to
their solution."[2] He goes on to repeat the major contentions
of his 1907 essay,[3] namely that religion and other cultural
institutions attempt to ameliorate the instinctual demands made
upon the individual by the requirements of culture.

> Our knowledge of the neurotic illnesses of individuals
> has been of much assistance to our understanding of
> the great social institutions. For the neuroses them-
> selves have turned out to be attempts to find *individ-
> ual* solutions for the problems of compensating for
> unsatisfied wishes, while the institutions seek to
> provide *social* solutions for these same problems.[4]

However, a number of contemporary analysts, e.g., Gedo and
Goldberg,[5] use the term, and since I should like to do so also,
it will be helpful to distinguish between a weak and a strong
use of it.

When it is used in a strong sense, "model" refers either
to a set of interrelated concepts, or mathematical propositions,
or to an artificial object which is designed to duplicate the
essential features of another object's relationships to its
environment. The obvious example of a physical object which
is rightly termed a model in the strong sense is the miniature
airplane flight engineers frequently use in wind tunnel tests
of wing designs.[6] Clearly, by using such models one hopes to
learn something one does not know or cannot easily investigate
about the object on which the model is based. The advantages
of such simulation are also obvious; by simulating poorly
understood systems we can learn a great deal about the real
object even if we fail to fully duplicate its essential features. If we simulate paranoia, for example,[7] and fail to convince expert witnesses, we have de facto learned something
about the logic and essential characteristics of that disease's

appearance. If we succeed in fooling expert witnesses, we gain important insights into the organizational relationships which must be a part of the structure of that disease. That is, if we successfully program a computer to answer questions put to it in such manner that psychiatrists cannot distinguish it from real human paranoid subjects, we need not conclude that the latter are nothing more than sophisticated computers. Rather, we can conclude that the organizational and functional relationships which obtain within the computer (the model) are systematically related to the organizational and functional relationships which obtain within the human subject.

> Resemblance in behavior of systems without identity of the inner systems is particularly feasible if the aspects in which we are interested arise out of the *organization* of the parts, independently of all but a few properties of the individual components.[8]

Minsky[9] offers a succinct definition of model which nicely illustrates the functional-pragmatic orientation the term conveys when used in the strong way.

> We use the term "model" in the following sense: To an observer B, an object A* is a model of an object A to the extent that B can use A* to answer questions that interest him about A.[10]

In short, when used in a strong sense, the term "model" refers to an object which we can manipulate, either physically or symbolically, in such a way that we can answer questions about and, in the most fortunate cases, make predictions about the behavior of the object of which it is a model.

When it is used in a weak sense, the term "model" refers to a high-level set of principles or theorems which organize and systematize lower level theorems and observations. Most psychoanalytic authors use the term in this weak sense. For example, in a recent book, *Models of the Mind*, the authors define model in this way:

> One common method of communicating a concept has been the construction of a model. A model is an ad hoc construction designed to make easier the understanding of complex, abstract theoretical propositions through the use of more easily encompassable pictorial or verbal analogies.[11]

When it is used in this weak sense one frequently finds it
interchanged with the term "theory," e.g., "...behaviors can be
understood using a variety of clinical theories or models of
the mind...."[12]

Rapaport uses the term in a similar way in his short
essay, "The Conceptual Model of Psychoanalysis." He suggests
that all the more complex psychoanalytic models of mental functioning are based upon the fundamental psychoanalytic
observation:

> restlessness (in infant)--appearance of breast and
> sucking--subsidence of restlessness.[13]

He goes on to suggest that the psychoanalytic theory of affective behavior is based upon this observational model, but

> ...it is not necessary that such a model be based on
> an *observational* sequence; it can well be based on a
> hypothetical construction, so long as it syste-
> matically coordinates the constructs to be used and
> holds out the hope that a realm of phenomena can
> rather completely be referred back to it.[14]

With the distinction between a strong and weak use of the
term in mind, I can now restate my general thesis and criticism
of Freud's psychology of religion to the extent that it depends
upon the formulations of the 1907 essay. In brief, my claim is
that in his clinical essays and in his metapsychological speculations on obsessional neurosis Freud consistently explains
that disease process in terms of the observational model Rapaport describes (hence "model" is used in the weak sense). But
when he examined cultural artifacts, such as religious rituals,
he used the various low-level clinical models as themselves,
high-level models for explaining and even predicting the various fate those behaviors might suffer, e.g., *The Future of an
Illusion*.

If this is correct, it has two serious implications for
our analysis of the rigor of Freud's interpretation of culture.
First, it seems logically suspect if, on the one hand, one
carefully avoids claiming too much rigor and predictive power
for one's system and, like Rapaport, only suggests that the
various models which make up that system are postdictive and

organizational and, on the other, attempts to use those very models to analyze and predict the future of much different and much more complex systems, as Freud does.

Second, if, as I have argued above, the equation between private obsessions and public rituals fails at its most crucial connection, the repression-suppression distinction, we rightly suspect that obsessional neurosis cannot serve as an adequate model of religious ritual, in either a strong or a weak sense.

In order to more fully illustrate these two significant features of Freud's psychology of religion, I will first review the (weak) model of obsessional neurosis he elaborated in his clinical essays, especially in the "Rat Man."[15] Then I shall try to show how he applied that model in a major text on religion, *Totem and Taboo*.

The Clinical Theory of Obsessional Neurosis, 1909-1913

Freud's major text on obsessional neurosis is the "Rat Man" case history he published in 1909. It is an extremely subtle text whose complexity is due not to the rigor of its theory but rather to the obscurities and confusion which the patient inadvertently forces upon the specific details of his story.[16] In fact, Freud is very hesitant to do more than hint at possible formulations and he offers very few "strong" hypotheses regarding the cause and disposition towards obsessional neurosis. This is not to say that he makes no theoretical claims. He quite openly admits that he sees no central, comprehensive model that will encompass the variety of clinical insights he derived from the case.

> ...starting out from this case, and also taking other cases into account which I have previously analysed, I shall make some disconnected statements of an aphoristic character upon the genesis and finer psychological mechanism of obsessional processes....[17]

He goes on to note that the phenomenology of obsessive thinking is inadequate,[18] and that he regards his propositions about the genesis of the disease to be no more than provisional formulations.[19]

This is an eminently just characterization for although he
uses the metapsychological (topographical) language of *The Interpretation of Dreams* he frequently avers to the variety of
defensive positions that an obsessive may assume against the
upsurge of libidinal drives. As we shall see when we examine
the entire set of metapsychological texts, the whole trend of
these formulations on defense and the person's reaction to sexual impulses intimates the later texts on the psychology of the
ego and the id. Indeed, Freud's closing thoughts on the case
may be read as direct precursors to the tripartite dissection
of the personality put forth fourteen years later in *The Ego
and the Id*.

> I cannot take leave of my patient without putting on
> my paper my impression that he had, as it were, dis-
> integrated into three personalities: into one uncon-
> scious personality [= id?], that is to say, and into
> two preconscious ones [= ego and superego?] between
> which his consciousness could oscillate. His uncon-
> scious comprised those of his impulses which had been
> suppressed at an early age and which might be de-
> scribed as passionate and evil impulses. In his
> normal state he was kind, cheerful, and sensible--
> an enlightened and superior kind of person--while in
> his third psychological organization he paid homage
> to superstition and asceticism.[20]

On the other hand, in an essay written a few years later,
he maintains the language of the instinct theory when he notes
that

> [there is the]...possibility that a chronological
> outstripping of libidinal development by ego develop-
> ment should be included in the disposition to obses-
> sional neurosis. A precocity of this kind would
> necessitate the choice of an object under the influ-
> ence of the ego-instincts, at a time at which the
> sexual instincts had not yet assumed their final
> shape, and a fixation at the stage of pregenital
> sexual organization would thus be left.[21]

The most significant example of such ego precocity is the
famous scene in which the patient, around the age of three,
having been punished by his deeply beloved father, hurls invec-
tives at him.

> ...he had done something naughty, for which his father
> gave him a beating. The little boy had flown into a

> terrible rage and had hurled abuse at his father even
> while he was under his blows. But as he knew no bad
> language, he had called him all the names of common
> objects that he could think of, and had screamed:
> "You lamp! You towel! You plate!" and so on. His
> father, shaken by such an outburst of elemental fury,
> had stopped beating him, and had declared: "The child
> will be either a great man or a great criminal!"[22]

Immediately following this rather marvelous outburst which, if
it were done on the stage, would be very comic, the boy drastically changed his character; "From that time forward he became a coward--out of fear of his own rage."[23] Freud concludes
that so sudden and dramatic a change of attitude could only be
accomplished by a massive reaction formation. In the face of
his own fury and the potential (castration threat) fury of his
much larger father, the boy's ego too efficiently repressed his
hatred which, at the full blossom of the late anal-sadistic
phase, was thereafter lost to adaptive ego control. But, as
Freud had already learned in his treatment of hysterics, such
massive repression[24] at so early an age means both that the
maturing personality is always deficient both in quantity and
quality of drive energies available to it and that the repressed
impulses will grow in the dark of the unconscious, where they
will take on even more frightening forms which must in turn be
continually repressed.

This massive early repression, then, sets the stage for
all later outbreaks of obsessional symptoms which invariably
symbolize, sometimes quite obviously, the return of the repressed hatred[25] that cannot be easily integrated with the
overt love that appears to dominate the obsessive's relationship to significant others; "We may regard the repression of
his infantile hatred of his father as the event which brought
his whole subsequent career under the dominion of the
neurosis."[26]

Early in the treatment, Freud made an especially insight-
ful observation which can be interpreted to offer additional
evidence supporting the notion that obsessive symptoms entail
a covert return of repressed impulses. Freud vividly describes
how his patient struggled to speak about a cruel story his captain had related to him. After begging Freud to let him

withhold the story, and after Freud gently tells him he cannot,
the patient chokingly describes the rat punishment. Freud
notes:

> At all the more important moments while he was telling
> his story his face took on a very strange, composite
> expression. I could only interpret it as one of
> *horror at pleasure of his own of which he himself was
> unaware.*[27]

The repressed wish, that such a thing might happen to his own
father, threatens to break through the repressive barrier and
therefore, as Freud will say at a later period, it promises
both the pleasure of instinctual discharge and the pleasure of
revenge. But, as I have already noted above, Freud implies
that the split that his patient manifests is twofold. Hence
there are three parts to his personality; the repressed which
enjoys the possibility of inflicting (and suffering?) such
punishment, the repressing part which is horrified at such a
wish, and the conscious part which is unaware of both the horror and the pleasure which his features exhibit.[28]

In other sections of the case history, Freud calls these
obsessional instances "deliria," a term similar to the more
typical "delusion."[29] However, the first term seems to more
adequately describe the experiential quality of his patient for
he himself recounts how puzzled he was at his own behavior.

> ...after working till far into the night, he used to
> go and open the front door to his father's ghost, and
> then look at his genitals in the looking-glass. *He
> tried to bring himself to his senses* by asking him-
> self what his father would say to it all if he were
> really still alive. But the argument had no effect
> so long as it was put forward in this rational shape.
> The spectre was not laid until he had transformed
> the same idea into a "delirious" threat to the effect
> that if he ever went through this nonsense again
> some evil would befall his father in the next world.[30]

Freud does not attempt to give more than metaphorical accounts of such delirious states, e.g., he says the disease
"grows bold enough to speak more plainly than before." Rather
he reverts back to his metapsychology of dreams and attempts to
explain the particular intensity of obsessive thoughts on the
basis of regression.

> A thought-process is obsessive or compulsive when, in
> consequence of an inhibition (due to a conflict of
> opposing impulses) at the motor end of the psychical
> system, it is undertaken with an expenditure of energy
> which (as regards both quality and quantity) is nor-
> mally reserved for actions alone; or, in other words,
> *an obsessive or compulsive thought is one whose func-*
> *tion is to represent an act regressively.*[31]

As we shall see when we examine Chapter VII of *The Inter-*
pretation of Dreams, this is the general, low-level, model with
which Freud explains a central mystery of dreams, namely,
"...the fact of their ideational contents being transformed
from thoughts into sensory images, to which belief is attached
and which appear to be experienced."[32] In both cases a thought
process (the dream wish, or the repressed obsessive desire) is
denied access to full-fledged expression, i.e., it cannot use
the motor apparatus. A dream wish cannot gain expression because the apparatus is shut down, as it were, during sleep.
But because of its intensity and the lack of external stimuli
it can elicit acts of endopsychic perception which in turn
create the delusion of actual perception.

In the same way an obsessive wish, for example, to kill
one's father, cannot gain expression because the secondary
system (ego) inhibits it with the variety of defensive maneuvers at its disposal. However, because of its intensity and
its relationship to the primal feelings of love and hate, it
sooner or later gains indirect expression, via obsessive
thoughts which, as we have seen, may elicit a kind of delu-
sional ("delirious") belief in one part of the personality.

Dreams and obsessive thoughts differ however in the important respect that the former are generally ego syntonic, while
the latter are not. In terms of the topographic model, this is
because obsessive thoughts may gain increasing dominance over
the psychological structures (ego) which control it.

Indeed, obsessive disorders typically manifest an increasing sexualization and aggressivization of formerly neutral behaviors. For example, Freud reports how his patient, while
studying for exams during the absence of his lady who was
nursing her grandmother, suddenly found himself thinking these
thoughts:

"If you received a command to take your examination
this term at the first possible opportunity, you might
manage to obey it. But if you were commanded to cut
your throat with a razor, what then?" He had at once
become aware that this command had already been given,
and was hurrying to the cupboard to fetch his razor
when he thought: "No, it's not so simple as that.
You must go and kill the old woman [his friend's
grandmother]." Upon that, he had fallen to the
ground, beside himself with horror.[33]

Freud reasons that secondary revision has reversed the order of
the actual sequence of wishes which had originally begun with
sexual longing for his lady, rage at her absence, death wishes
toward the old woman who kept her away, and the subsequent command to commit suicide, "Kill yourself, as a punishment for
these savage and murderous passions!"[34]

Having breifly reviewed this elegant case history--Freud
reports a complete cure in eleven months--we may summarize the
main features of the weak model of obsessional neurosis Freud
advances there.

1. There is an early, generally pre-oedipal, efflores-
   cence of sexual behavior, especially voyeurism of
   older siblings and family members.

2. A traumatic encounter occurs in which very strong
   hatred is roused against a parent or parent figure.

3. Those very strong feelings are checked, often because of castration and instinctual anxiety, by
   excessively rigid defensive postures.

4. The repressed aggressive impulses may return in
   early childhood, and be warded off by obsessive-
   compulsive defenses, e.g., magic.

5. At puberty and other times of especially intense
   sexual pressure, obsessive features reemerge to
   counteract the surge of sexual and repressed
   aggressive impulses that are awakened.

6. Decomposition frequently occurs:

   "True obsessional acts...are only made possible
   because they constitute a kind of reconciliation,
   in the shape of a compromise, between the two
   antagonistic impulses. For obsessional acts
   tend to approximate more and more--and the
   longer the disorder lasts the more evident does
   this become--to infantile acts of a masturbatory
   character."[35]

7. The obsessive frequently recognizes the absurdity
   of his actions and rituals, but he is quite unable
   to stop them except by elaborating additional protective formulae. Thus while he manifests ignorance of the force of his hatred, he may think out
   loud the most murderous and horrible thoughts.
   He behaves and experiences himself as if he were
   two distinct personalities, e.g., the Rat Man's
   sudden compulsion to cut his throat.[36]

When we examine Freud's major texts on religion, I should
like to put two questions to them: (1) What is the status of
the psychopathological model, obsessional neurosis, he uses to
interpret them? (2) Do the various religious phenomena he examines manifest any or all these seven major features of obsessional neurosis?

Totem and Taboo: The Weak Model Applied

Freud began compiling materials on social psychology and
anthropology of primitives early in 1910, just three years
after the publication of the 1907 essay on religious acts and
obsessions. Following somewhat in the footsteps of Wundt,[37]
who applied nonanalytic psychology to myths and rites, and
Jung,[38] who in Freud's words used social psychology to explain
individual myths, Freud made the status of his claims very
clear.

It will be found that the two principal themes from
which the title of this little book is derived--
totems and taboos--have not received the same treatment. The analysis of taboos is put forward as an
assured and exhaustive attempt at the solution of
the problem. The investigation of totemism does
not more than declare that "here is what psycho-
analysis can at the moment contribute to elucidating
the problem of the totem."[39]

He explains this disparity by noting that taboos still
exist among us while totemism is more or less alien to modern
life. Now while he observes a customary diffidence about
applying psychology to nonpsychological materials, that is
ethnographical reports, he also makes two very strong claims
about the implied equation of private obsession and public
taboo; (1) that by studying the former he can completely

explain the latter, and (2) that "taboos persist among us,"
i.e., in the actions of obsessive neurotics. In other words,
the weak clinical model of obsessive compulsive neurosis becomes, in this essay in applied psychoanalysis, a strong model
for interpreting cultural "obsessive neurosis": religion.

In the first chapter, "The Horror of Incest," he speculates about the origins of totemism, using anthropological
theories, i.e., Frazer and Lang, which were unpopular even then.
For example, he quotes Frazer's contention that "an Australian's
relation to his totem is the basis of all his social obliga-
tions...."[40] After reviewing a series of field studies, speculations, and a great deal of material from Frazer, he concludes
with the comparatively minor claim that we can see in the unconscious of savage races incest taboos and incest longings
which are strikingly similar to those we see in neurotics.

True to his word, Freud levels his strongest arguments in
favor of the hypothesis that religion is a public-neurosis in
his two middle chapters, "Taboo and Emotional Experience" and
"Animism, Magic and the Omnipotence of Thoughts." After reviewing the range of definitions of "taboo,"[41] Freud says that,
at first glance, the trained psychoanalyst might well call obsessive compulsive neurosis "taboo illness."[42] He duly notes
that the analogy which he intends to draw between obsessive
compulsive neurosis and religious behaviors (taboo) may be
based upon superficial rather than fundamental similarities.
Nevertheless, he goes on to compare the two phenomena and then
summarizes his findings.

> Let us now summarize the points in which agreement
> between taboo usages and obsessional symptoms is most
> clearly shown: (1) the fact that the prohibitions
> lack any assignable motive; (2) the fact that they
> are maintained by an internal necessity; (3) the
> fact that they are easily displaceable and that there
> is risk of infection from the prohibited object; and
> (4) the fact that they give rise to injunctions for
> the performance of ceremonial acts.[43]

A few pages later he notes that he is using obsessive
compulsive neurosis as a strong model and that therefore he
must show how it illuminates an otherwise obscure or

unrecognized feature of taboo.[44] That obscure feature is emotional ambivalence which he claims to find in at least three
major forms of primitive rituals; the treatment of enemies, the
highly ambivalent status of kings, and the nearly universal
taboos upon the dead.[45] Indeed he goes on to speculate that
the term "taboo" itself may, like other archaic words have been
from the beginning, express contrary meanings and that "...from
the very first it was used to designate a particular kind of
ambivalence and whatever arose from it."[46]

In addition, we find, according to Freud, that taboo behavior manifests both a tendency toward a decomposition and a
basis in repression. We see the former in those numerous cases
in which a person who violates a taboo himself becomes taboo.
Why? Because by violating a taboo he awakens in others an echo
of their own repressed desires to accomplish the same strin-
gently forbidden act; "...he is truly contagious in that every
example encourages imitation, and for that reason he himself
must be shunned."[47] In the same way even persons such as
widows who are innocent of any violations may become taboo because otherwise they may incite others to commit offenses.
Thus just as the lonely neurotic must shore up his failing defenses by more and more restrictive prohibitions and rituals,
so too a group endangered by taboo violation will increase its
vigilance by increasing the "jurisdiction" of taboo and the
frequency of expiatory acts. Also, the presence of expiatory
acts following taboo violation supports the hypothesis that
renunciation (or repression) of primal wishes is the heart of
taboo.

> Emancipation from one renunciation is made up for by
> the imposition of another one elsewhere. This leads
> us to conclude that atonement is a more fundamental
> factor than purification in the ceremonials of
> taboo.[48]

That taboos are erected upon or through a series of acts
of repression follows from two assertions whose logical status
differ.

The first is that, in many cases, the native informant
cannot explain why a particular thing is taboo.

> The most obvious and striking point of agreement
> between the obsessional prohibitions of neurotics
> and taboos is that these prohibitions are equally
> lacking in motive and equally puzzling in their
> origin. Having made their appearance at some un-
> specified moment, they are forcibly maintained by
> an irresistible fear.[49]

Of course this is not a very solid argument for, again
allowing Freud the rhetorical point that taboo behaviors may
appear strange to an outsider, or lacking in motive, he gives
very little evidence that they are so to the natives themselves.
His rationalist bias shows through for he clearly means to say
that the myths, legends, stories, and other possible explanations for taboo which many native cultures use to explain their
"puzzling" behavior can only be secondary revisions, since they
are so unscientific and irrational.

The second, and much more basic, assertion which supports
the repression hypothesis is the rather circular one that the
model requires it.[50]

> ...it must be said that there is no sense in asking
> savages to tell us the real reason for their
> prohibitions--the origin of taboo. It follows from
> our postulates that they cannot answer, since their
> real reason must be "unconscious." We can, however,
> reconstruct the history of taboo as follows on the
> model of obsessional prohibitions.[51]

However, granting him this postulate, we must still ask if the
prohibitions and restrictions that characterize the imposition
of taboos are the results of repression or suppression. As I
have tried to show above, these two terms designate quite distinct processes; the former entails or implies the presence of
psychopathology, the latter only implies the presence of instinct control. Freud does not directly address himself to
this question. He consistently describes taboos as prohibitions. But he consistently implies that they are essentially
repressive for repression is the most fundamentally primitive
response to instinctual demands. Primitive peoples, according
to Freud's sources, manifest typical features of repressed personalities; they are ignorant of their real motives for their
sexual and aggressive behavior, their prohibitions are strin-
gent, severe, and irrational and are subject to many of those

primary process modes, e.g., displacement, condensation, symbolization, which are characteristic of repressed impulses.
Finally, and most importantly, primitives themselves act out
intense and usually unconscious ambivalence toward significant
persons. This too is characteristic of repressed personalities.[52]

If we add the presence of repression, tendency to decomposition, and intense ambivalence to Freud's list of the similarities between obsessional neurosis and taboo behavior, we
find that it now includes the seven features of obsessional
neurosis we derived from our reading of the Rat Man case history.

While he is aware of the speculative nature of his propositions, Freud also recognizes that he really aims to reconstruct
the childhood of the race on the basis of his clinical knowledge
of the childhood of his neurotic patients; "These are no more
than hints, but if they were attentively developed their importance for our understanding of the growth of civilization would
become apparent."[53]

He does concede that in their contemporary forms, religious
rituals and neurotic obsessional acts are, on the manifest level,
quite distinct. However, he goes on to argue, this is so not
because they are fundamentally different but because they have
the same origins and distinct developmental histories. In comparing the salient features of obsessional neurosis with those
of taboo behavior, Freud clearly means to say that they are
both essentially the kind of behavior typical of the earliest
phases of human development, both on the ontogenetic and phylogenetic levels. Thus a neurotic is someone who, for constitu-
tional or environmental reasons, fails to achieve the level of
self-control and integrated expressiveness (ego development)
which society as a whole requires of him and of itself. Every
child must relive in a few short years and reaccomplish those
developmental tasks his society has accomplished over many
centuries.

> We need not discuss here how this alteration came
> about or how much share in it is due to a constitu-
> tional modification and how much to a real improve-
> ment in family relations. But this example suggests
> the probability that *the psychical impulses of*

primitive peoples were characterized by a higher
amount of ambivalence than is to be found in modern
civilized man.   It is to be supposed that as this
ambivalence diminished, taboo (a symptom of the
ambivalence and a compromise between the two con-
flicting impulses) slowly disappeared. Neurotics,
who are obliged to reproduce the struggle and the
taboo resulting from it, may be said to have in-
herited an archaic constitution as an atavistic
vestige; the need to compensate for this at the
behest of civilization is what drives them to their
immense expenditure of mental energy.[54]

In other words, neurotics are throwbacks to an earlier,
developmentally-prior, condition typical of the race itself.
Thus religion and obsessional neurosis share a genetic identity which, in the famous passage of *The Future of an Illusion*,
leads Freud to suggest that contemporary vestiges of the former
will, under rational, scientific analysis, disappear just as
the latter does within the confines of the psychoanalytic
relationship.

Contrary to appearances, Freud is not simply proposing
that he has uncovered a striking analogy between private neuroses and religious or totemic practices. Rather, he means to
show that the two have identical roots in universal conflicts.
Thus he must raise and attempt to answer the historical question: When and how did the intense primal ambivalence characteristic of primitive minds disappear from normal social life?
He answers by concocting out of a heterogeneous group of theories the ill-famed story of the primal horde which is essentially the Oedipus complex recast as an outright dramatic event.
Thus the primal father may have actually been castrating, the
primal sons openly desired their mothers and sisters as sexual
objects, and the sons gathered together finally to overthrow
their tyrannous father. The whole force of his argument requires Freud to conclude that these were concrete events.

An event such as the elimination of the primal father
by the company of his sons must inevitably have left
ineradicable traces in the history of humanity; and
the less it itself was recollected, the more numerous
must have been the substitutes to which it gave rise.[55]

Again, Freud's attempts to reconstruct the origins of
totemic behavior are much more than essays in applied

psychoanalysis in which he hoped to illuminate some obscurities
in anthropological data by analogies drawn from psychoanalytic
practice.[56] On the contrary, *Totem and Taboo* entails a twofold
project; Freud wished to demonstrate the applicability of the
clinical theory he had advanced in the Rat Man case history to
larger, nonclinical enterprises, and at the same time, he wished
to support the clinical theory with the evidence presented in
Totem and Taboo.

While much of his argument is entirely circular it has the
merits of a kind of self-reflection that allows Freud to revert
back to the formerly clear case of obsessional neurosis with
the new "evidence" that his forays into anthropology had gained
for him.

> Let us, then, examine more closely the case of
> neurosis....It is not accurate to say that obses-
> sional neurotics, weighed down under the burden of
> an excessive morality, are definding themselves
> only against *psychological* reality and are punishing
> themselves for impulses which were merely *felt*.
> *Historical* reality has a share in the matter as well.
> In their childhood they had these evil impulses pure
> and simple, and turned them into acts so far as the
> impotence of childhood allowed.[57]

In summary, what had been a weak clinical model of obsessional neurosis in the 1909 case history became in *Totem and
Taboo*, and in all of Freud's subsequent works on cultural forms,
a strong model with which he sought to explain both the history
and predict the future of religion itself. In the final paragraph to the book Freud reveals this design quite openly.[58]

> Primitive men...are *uninhibited*: thought passes
> directly into action. With them it is rather the
> deed that is a substitute for the thought. And that
> is why, without laying claims to any finality of
> judgement, I think that in the case before us it may
> safely be assumed that "in the beginning was the
> Deed."[59]

It is perhaps no accident that Freud should end his archeology
of religion with this famous quotation from Goethe's *Faust* for
the play as a whole is as critical of religious orthodoxy, especially theological pretensions, as Freud himself was throughout his life.[60]

Thus Freud rounds out his myth of the origin of culture, which includes an explanation of the central Christian mystery, the Eucharist, by referring back to Goethe's often anti-Christian masterpiece as an indirect proof text of the legitimacy of his speculations. Indeed, he uses Goethe again to explicate a central feature of the theory of the original crime which, as we have seen, is first detected in repressed fantasies that in turn lead us back to uncover the original, historical, deed each of us obscurely recalls in our own unconscious.

> ...I have supposed that the sense of guilt for an action has persisted for many thousands of years and has remained operative in generations which can have had no knowledge of that action. I have supposed that an emotional process, such as might have developed in generations of sons who were ill-treated by their father, has extended to new generations which were exempt from such treatment....[61]

This presents a problem unless one is willing to suppose that such complex feeling-toned memories can be passed on through some kind of group mind.

> A part of the problem seems to be met by the inheritance of psychical dispositions which, however, need to be given some sort of impetus in the life of the individual before they can be roused into actual operation. This may be the meaning of the poet's words:
>
> *Was du ererbt von deinen Vätern hast,*
> *Erwirb es, um es zu besitzen.*
>
> ["What thou has inherited from thy fathers, acquire and make it thine."][62]

Obviously Freud could have stated his thesis more baldly and forsook the references to *Faust*. That he did not, that he wrote the entire text so carefully and with such attention to literary form, and with so little attention to factual incongruities, supports my contention that the weak model of obsessional neurosis became much more of a pre-text for the speculations that appear in the end of *Totem and Taboo*.

NOTES

CHAPTER II

[1]H. A. Simon, *The Sciences of the Artificial* (Cambridge: MIT Press, 1969).

[2]Freud, "Claims of Psycho-Analysis," 185.

[3]These appear in other short papers of that period: "'Civilized' Sexual Morality and Modern Nervous Illness," *SE* 9 (1959 [1908d]) 179-204; "The Antithetical Meaning of Primal Words," *SE* 11 (1957 [1910e]) 155-161; "The Significance of Vowel Sequences," *SE* 12 (1958 [1911d]) 341; "Great is Diana of the Ephesians," *SE* 12 (1958 [1911f]) 342-344; "Postscript to the Case of Paranoia," *SE* 12 (1958 [1912a]) 80-82; "The Occurrence in Dreams of Material from Fairy Tales," *SE* 12 (1958 [1913d]) 281-287; "The Theme of the Three Caskets," *SE* 12 (1958 [1913f]) 291-301; "Preface to J. G. Bourke's *Scatalogic Rites of All Nations*," *SE* 12 (1958 [1913k]) 335-337.

[4]Freud, "Claims of Psycho-Analysis," 186.

[5]John E. Gedo and Arnold Goldberg, *Models of the Mind* (Chicago: University of Chicago, 1973).

[6]With the advent of the computer age, one can do the same thing without having to construct an actual physical model. By programming a sufficiently accurate description of the proposed aircraft and wind conditions into the computer, one can carry out a simulation of a simulation. See H. A. Simon, *The Sciences of the Artificial* (14-15) where he describes early attempts to actually construct a hydraulic model of a Keynesian economy.

[7]See the short article, "The Paranoid Computer," *Scientific American* 228 (February 1973) 48-49.

[8]Simon, *Sciences of the Artificial*, 17.

[9]M. L. Minsky, "Matter, Mind, and Models," pp. 45-49 in *Proceedings of the International Federation of Information Processing Congress* 1 (Washington, DC: Spartan, 1965).

[10]Ibid., 45.

[11]Gedo and Goldberg, *Models of the Mind*, 3-4.

[12]Ibid., 7.

[13]He bases this upon Chapter VII of *The Interpretation of Dreams* and the 1911 essay on mental functioning; see Sigmund Freud, "Formulations on the Two Principles of Mental Functioning," *SE* 12 (1958 [1911b]) 215-226. See also David Rapaport, "The Conceptual Model of Psychoanalysis," p. 409 in *The*

Collected Papers of David Rapaport (ed. Merton Gill; New York:
Basic Books, 1967).

[14]Rapaport, "Conceptual Model," 410.

[15]Sigmund Freud, "Notes upon a Case of Obsessional
Neurosis," *SE* 10 (1955 [1909d]) 155-318.

[16]Gedo and Goldberg provide a useful summary of the case.
The patient was a twenty-nine-year-old lawyer who had suffered
from obsessional symptoms since early childhood. For over four
years he had had intense fears of harming either his father or
a woman he admired; he also had impulses to cut his own throat.
The struggle against his obsessions was increasingly impoverish-
ing his professional and personal life. His difficulties had
come to a head during army maneuvers the summer prior to seeking treatment in 1907. He became obsessed with the fantasy
that his father and beloved lady would be subjected to a tor-
ture he had heard of which involved rats eating their way into
the victim's anus. This idea was warded off by means of magical formulas made up of words or gestures which eventuated in
ceremonials of repetitive doing and undoing.
     The patient's earliest memories related to the death of
an older sister who had been very close to him, and to an at-
tack of rage against his father. These were events from the
fourth or fifth year of his life. He recalled having intense
sexual curiosity around the same ages. By the age of six he
had developed the feeling that his voyeuristic wishes would
kill his father. In order to prevent the father's demise, he
had to set up compulsive rituals to undo the effects of his
scoptophilic wishes. Similar obsessions recurred when, at the
age of twenty, he fell in love with his cousin. Remarkably,
these fears persisted in spite of the fact that his father
actually died when the patient was twenty-one. The exacerba-
tion of the obsessions that preceded the analysis had followed
rejection by his cousin and the emergence of a plan to marry
another woman (*Models of the Mind*, 28-29).

[17]Freud, "Notes upon a Case of Obsessional Neurosis," 155.

[18]Ibid., 222.

[19]Ibid., 244.

[20]Ibid., 248.

[21]Sigmund Freud, "The Disposition to Obsessional Neurosis,"
SE 12 (1958 [1913i]) 325.

[22]Idem, "Notes upon a Case of Obsessional Neurosis," 205.

[23]Ibid., 206.

[24]In this text and in all texts up to the 1926 essay *Inhibitions, Symptoms and Anxiety,* Freud often uses the terms
"repression" and "defense" interchangeably. Thus he will speak
of two kinds of repression ("Notes upon a Case of Obsessional

Neurosis," 196), when in effect he means to speak of two kinds of defense. The "Rat Man" case history is studded with casual references to a large variety of defenses, including displacement, denial, negation, distortion, symbolization, undoing, insolation, regression, and inhibition; see Strachey's index for page references, *SE* 10.329-342. Cf. *Totem and Taboo* where he describes ritual mourning as based on "the repression of the unconscious hostility by the method of projection..." (Sigmund Freud, *Totem and Taboo*, *SE* 13 [1953 (1912-13)] 63).

[25]Thus the young man denied his own rage at his father, and both projected and displace it onto the captain who he says was not a bad man but clearly seemed very fond of cruelty ("Notes upon a Case of Obsessional Neurosis," 166). Freud's interpretation that the captain very clearly serves as a transference object for the young man seems unimpeachable when we learn that the latter's fear of the former began after they had disagreed over the justness of corporal punishment (166). In the original notes to the case, Freud notes that he "...pointed out to him that this attempt to deny the reality of his father's death is the basis of his whole neurosis" (300).

[26]Ibid., 238.

[27]Ibid., 166-167.

[28]V. Tausk ("Compensation as a Means of Discounting the Motive of Repression," *International Journal of Psycho-Analysis* 5 [1924] 130-140) also addressed himself to this question and he noted one frequently finds that in the long line of associations which lead from an initial blocking to finally recovering the repressed idea the terminal associations are pleasurable and seem to console the patient for the pain he is about to experience; "[Such an association] acts as an antidote to the motive for repression, and permits restitution of the memory by setting the greater strength of the present and better hope for the future against the weak and feeble past" (137).

[29]Freud, "Notes upon a Case of Obsessional Neurosis," 164 n. 1.

[30]Ibid., 222-223 (my italics).

[31]Ibid., 246.

[32]Freud, *Interpretation of Dreams*, 535.

[33]Idem, "Notes upon a Case of Obsessional Neurosis," 187.

[34]Ibid., 188.

[35]Ibid., 244.

[36]Ibid., 229.

[37]W. Wundt, *Völkerpsychologie*, Vol. 2, Part II, *Mythus und Religion* (Leipzig, 1906).

[38]C. Jung, *Wandlungen und Symbole der Libido* (Leipzig: Deuticke, 1912).

[39]Freud, *Totem and Taboo*, xiii-xiv.

[40]Ibid., 3; J. G. Frazer, *Totemism and Exogamy* 1 (4 vols.; London: Macmillan, 1910) 53.

[41]He settles on one which fully stresses the ambiguous ways in which the term may be used: "The meaning of 'taboo,' as we see it, diverges in two contrary directions. To us it means, on the one hand, 'sacred,' 'consecrated,' and on the other, 'uncanny,' 'dangerous,' 'forbidden,' 'unclean'" (*Totem and Taboo*, 18).

[42]Ibid., 26.

[43]Ibid., 28-29.

[44]"If...we could succeed in demonstrating that ambivalence, that is, the dominance of opposing trends, is also to be found in the observances of taboo, or if we could point to some of them which, like obsessional acts, give simultaneous expression to both currents, we should have established the psychological agreement between taboo and obsessional neurosis in what is perhaps their most important feature" (*Totem and Taboo*, 36). He even uses the term "model"; see below, n. 50.

[45]Ibid., 36-64.

[46]Ibid., 67.

[47]Ibid., 32.

[48]Ibid.,,34.

[49]Ibid., 26.

[50]By "model of obsessional prohibitions" (Sigmund Freud, *Vorbild der Zwangsverbote*, p. 41 in *Gesammelte Werke* 9 [18 vols.; London: Imago Publishing Co., 1940-1968]; hereafter cited as *GW*), Freud means of course the low level clinical theory which he had worked out most fully in the Rat Man case history. As I have suggested above, in order to accomplish this Freud must rather dramatically increase the predictive (or post-dictive) status of that clinical theory. He also must add a rather central proviso that "taboos...were at some time externally imposed upon a generation of primitive men; they must, that is to say, no doubt have been impressed on them violently by the previous generation." Freud must insist upon this supposition; without it the model fails for he must explain the origins of the "repression" which the clinical theory requires us to ascribe to the cultural neurosis of taboo.

[51]Idem, *Totem and Taboo*, 31.

[52]"Anyone who investigates the origin and significance of dreams of the death of loved relatives (of parents or brothers and sisters) will be able to convince himself that as dreamers, children and savages are at one in their attitude towards the dead--an attitude based upon emotional ambivalence" (Freud, *Totem and Taboo*, 62).

[53]Ibid., 71.

[54]Ibid., 66.

[55]Ibid., 155.

[56]H. Kohut, *The Analysis of the Self* (New York: International Universities Press) 254-255.

[57]Freud, *Totem and Taboo*, 160-161.

[58]This is not to say that he failed to see any difference between neurotic and cultural forms of obsessive actions. Rather he repeats, more or less, the claims he had made in the 1907 essay regarding the nature of the instincts which are characteristically associated with each form. In cultural artifacts, such as ritual acts, the associated instincts are social, while "...*the fact which is characteristic of the neurosis is the preponderance of the sexual over the social instinctual elements*. The social instincts [*Die sozialen Triebe*], however, are themselves derived from a combination of egoistic and erotic components into wholes of a special kind" (Freud, *Totem and Taboo*, 73; *GW*, 9.91). However, Freud never explains how these surely very important instincts are special, nor their origins. At the time of the composition of *Totem and Taboo*, "social instinct" and "ego instinct" were not metapsychologically grounded nor did they have clinical status. They served, rather, to explain, in instinct terms, the reality of an intrapsychic and interpersonal conflict in the lives of neurotics and, by extension, primitives.

[59]Freud, *Totem and Taboo*, 161.

[60]These appear as lines 1224-1237 in W. Kaufmann, *Goethe's Faust* (Garden City, NY: Anchor Books, Doubleday, 1961) 153; Freud, *Totem and Taboo*, 161, n. 1.

[61]Freud, *Totem and Taboo*, 157-158.

[62]Ibid., 158, n. 1.

CHAPTERS III

RITUAL ACTIONS AND THE COMPULSION TO REPEAT

Having examined the origins and history of Freud's analogy
between ritual actions and obsessive behaviors and the way in
which he used that analogy in his grand critique of religion,
we can ask, is there more to say? Did Freud exhaust the interpretive possibilities of his own metapsychology in his essays
on religion? In the two previous chapters, I have tried to
indicate that the proper answer to this question is no. If I
am correct in arguing that Freud's fundamental critique of
religion is not supported by his own metapsychological formulations, it seems reasonable to reexamine the development of the
metapsychology and see if, working within the theory itself, we
can find materials there which might ultimately contribute to a
more comprehensive psychoanalytic theory of ritual behavior.

But, in order to begin that task we must first formulate a
concise, psychologically neutral, definition of ritual that
neither sins on the side of reductionism nor floats away in the
too faint air of abstraction. With such a definition in hand
we can then readdress the metapsychological essays and examine
how each of them in turn explains some or all of the component
concepts of our neutral definition.[1]

Because Freud failed to develop his psychology of ritual
in light of his developing clinical theory, and because he
wrote with a particular close-mindedness about religion, in
order to use his theories in an other than hostile evaluation
of religion one must first confront the master and wrest his
concepts away from him.

With that task in mind, I propose to examine his most
speculative metapsychological essay, *Beyond the Pleasure Principle*. This essay is an especially attractive entry point for
a reexamination of the metapsychology of ritual for two reasons.
First, in it Freud discusses and attempts to explain certain
behaviors (e.g., children's play) which seem similar to ritual
behavior as I describe that phenomenon in the first part of
this chapter. Second, as I shall try to demonstrate, the

39

extremely agile yet ultimately unconvincing way in which he
employs metapsychological principles to show that there is a
tendency in life which is "beyond" the pleasure principle allows
us to uncover the girders of his argument without adopting the
contorted structure of his conclusions. With those girders,
that is, those more fundamental metapsychological formulations,
in hand we can reexamine their individual and collective history in the various phases of the development of the metapsychology.

In this chapter I should like to accomplish these three
goals: (1) formulate a neutral definition of ritual behavior;
(2) examine the arguments in *Beyond the Pleasure Principle* in
light of this definition; and, (3) abstract from that essay
the metapsychological formulations which are most relevant to
explaining ritual behavior.

Ritual: Definitions and Conceptual Problems

The way in which one defines the term "ritual" directly
influences the development of one's subsequent analysis of the
phenomenon.

Frequently, definitions offered by psychologists and
sociologists are part and parcel of the author's theory of
religious behavior. Thus after setting forth the grand dichotomies of sacred and profane, Durkheim defines ritual as "the
rules of conduct which prescribe how a man should comport himself in the presence of these sacred objects."[2]

Freud's discussion of obsessive acts and ritual clearly
presupposes his economic theory of the origins of social life;
culture requires energy for its operations and it leaches that
energy out of the instinctual supplies of its members who, in
turn, adjudicate and adjust their conflict with the forces of
culture through symptomatic rituals. Other authors[3] use the
term "ritual" to describe behavior not usually associated with
religious practices, e.g., "Ritual...is prescribed formal behavior for occasions not given over to technological routine."[4]

The virtue of these latter definitions of ritual is that
they are theoretically simpler and so less distant from

observation than those of Durkheim and Freud quoted above.
Lukes is quite aware of these difficulties and he offers the
following minimal definition.

> Ritual: rule-governed activity of a symbolic character
> which draws the attention of its participants to ob-
> jects of thought and feeling which they hold to be of
> special significance.[5]

By "rule governed," Lukes means that rituals generally are
patterned, repetitious, behaviors which carry a "normative
pressure" on their adherents. While he does not clarify what
normative pressure means, I assume he wants to suggest that
ritual actors have a psychological awareness of rightness and
wrongness in their performance and it is, in part, this awareness which maintains the patterned form of the ritual.

By "symbolic" character, Lukes means to follow Parsons[6]
and later authors such as Sperber[7] who distinguish symbolic
activity from means-end activity; symbolic activity is activity
which is in itself meaningful and efficacious, while means-end
activity is behavior oriented toward the accomplishment of a
goal which is extrinsic to the behavior.

The last part of Lukes' definition, that rituals pertain
to objects about which the participants have special feelings,
follows from the implicit evaluative quality of the notion
"normative pressure." Obviously this is a very fuzzy notion--
how special must the object or one's feelings about it be?
However, it does seem that both in ordinary use and in scholarly discussions, the terms "ritual" or "ritualized" imply that
the act in question or the objects to which it pertains are of
an extraordinary nature.

Following Lukes' discussion and in light of other definitions of the term "ritual," we can isolate five salient features of the concept "ritual," and hence, by extension, of the
various phenomena given that name. Ritual is

> human (or animal) activity
> repetitive (or patterned)
> functional (or "meaningful")
> symbolic (or representational)
> normative

There are a number of questions we may ask about each of
these conceptual features that will help us construct an adequate theory of ritual.

First, how operational must our definition of ritual behavior be? Since ritual is behavior, and behavior is what
people do, does it follow that an adequate definition of ritual
should enable us to examine another person's or group's behavior and, without native informants, correctly designate their
"rituals"? We may forego carrying out the requested thought
experiment and simply note that the last three elements on our
list (functional, symbolic, and normative) all entail our knowing something--actually a good deal--about the beliefs, conceptions, and "feelings" of the people whose rituals we observe.
It seems clear that while all human beings sleep every twenty-
four hours or so, not all of them ritualize going to bed and
getting up. To say that someone ritualizes going to bed is to
say something about his "state of mind," his disposition and
his beliefs.

A central feature of rituals is their conservativeness.
Unlike the stories, myths, and theologies which may or may not
accompany them, they change very little and very slowly. It
was the persistence of ritual forms over extended periods of
time that led Jane Harrison to conclude that rite is prior to
and more fundamental than myth.[8] This leads us to ask why
ritual forms persist longer and with less change than the
myths-theologies which accompany them.

The persistence of ritual forms and the apparent primacy
of those forms over linguistic-intellectual formulas (myths and
theologies) suggests that at least some of the substructure of
ritual forms is based upon or represents biological or
structural-psychological elements which are both more rigid and
less susceptible to change than are intellectual products.
Leach,[9] among many others, notes that one may find, within the
same natuve population, quite distinct and logically incom-
patible explanations and theological accounts of the significance of a ritual form which is common to the population as a
whole.

The fact that native informants, just as their counterpart
experts in our culture, do differ in their interpretations of
the significance of a particular ritual ought to make us wary
when we attempt to isolate the functional (meaning) significance of that ritual. Indeed, it might be that the term "functional" is too strong for it implies that the act in question
actually does perform some function whose absence would be
apparent. It is conceivable that a particular ritual has no
such function and that, should the usual performers put it
aside for some reason, it would not be missed. This is a dis-
quieting proposition to most theorists of ritual for they too
assume that behaviors that have persisted over centuries, as
is the case of certain Christian and Jewish religious rituals
for example, must have some relevant role or "function" in
those societies where they appear. No doubt they are correct.
But, it seems in order to fully justify this functional hypothesis one would want to show the more or less "counter-
productive" or dysfunctional effects the absence of the ritual
in question would have upon its traditional environment. While
it seems reasonable to agree with those authors who stress the
functional properties of ritual, it does not seem necessary to
maintain the strong position that the absence of such rituals
would necessarily bring about dysfunctioning. To maintain this
strong position is to predict the outcome of an event which,
in the case of complex social relations, has innumerable
variables.

To say that an action is functional is to say that it is
neither an accident, nor simply a matter of habit, nor immediately dispensable. To put it positively, to have a function
is to have a more or less important task or job to perform in
a larger operation. Thus to perform a function is to exert
force within a field of forces.[10]

The notion of a field of forces or energies which are ex-
pended in ritual processes is basic to the major discussions of
ritual behavior in psychoanalytic theory, ethology, and sociology.[11] While theories like these represent different levels
of abstraction, it seems fair to ask of each of them, and of

ourselves, when we propose a model of ritual behavior, the
following questions.

> How are we to conceive of the field of forces?
> How do these forces interact and affect one another?
> What is the systematic relationship which must hold
>   between these forces such that it makes sense to
>   speak of "function"?
> How precisely may we quantify and measure these
>   forces?[12]

As Lukes, Leach, and Hollis[13] note in their discussions of
the symbolic nature of ritual, behaviors which the investigator
cannot otherwise account for in rational, economic, or usually
means-end explanation are often by default termed "symbolic."
Obviously this is not a sufficiently clear method. The underlying logic of its application seems to be that symbolic actions (e.g., rituals) are actions performed in the absence of
a better way to accomplish the desired aim. Not only does this
notion of symbol raise complex questions about our knowledge of
the ritual performer's beliefs (does he himself believe that
his actions are "indirect"?), but it entails the judgment that
rituals are finally weak-kneed attempts at action.

A more useful approach is to examine the notion of symbol
along three dichotomous axes: (1) latent-manifest, (2) signi-
fier-signified, and (3) speech-action.

The distinction between latent and manifest meanings of a
symbol is basic to psychoanalytic hermeneutics.[14] Briefly, it
asserts that particular symbols, whether in dreams or appearing
in myths, are symptomatic expression of more fundamental impulses (e.g., the urge to investigate the sexual organs of
another person versus the awareness of danger which that
brings about) that conflict with each other and which conflict
is mitigated by the ego's production of the compromise formation, the symbol-symptom.

In order to maintain this notion of symbol, one would
then have to follow Freud's example[15] and attempt to designate
both the latent (unconscious, repressed, or suppressed) wish
and the manifest danger which brought about the need for symbolism or disguise. Jones states the extreme case.

Only what is repressed is symbolized; only what is
repressed needs to be symbolized. This conclusion is
the touchstone of the psychoanalytic theory of
symbolism.[16]

The limitations of this extreme position are discussed by
Ricoeur.[17] The major defect he points out in the narrow analytic notion of symbol is that sexual terms and experience are
always held to be primary (both ontogenetically and phylogenetically) to all other forms and content. By equating symbols
with symptoms, Freud necessarily implies that symbols are always second-order expressions, that they are expressions born
in fear and shaped by repression. Ricoeur instead prefers to
examine symbols in terms of the distinction (derived from linguistics) between signifier and signified.[18]

In order to make this distinction, one must be able to
stand apart from the relationship between signifier and signified and so judge, as it were, the fact that they are so linked.
When the signifier is a word or linguistic unit and the signified is an object (e.g., a human being), it is possible to isolate both halves of the linkage. We can also do this with non-
linguistic signs; we can observe the systematic variance which
the presence or absence of a particular sign causes in a particular context, e.g., flashing light above an intersection.
In the same way, we can observe how the presence or absence of
certain tail coloration in ducks acts as a sign of the sexual
availability of that duck to other ducks.[19]

Can we do the same for a particular ritual? That is, can
we isolate both the ritual behavior under study and that-which-
it-signifies and observe what effects performance or non-
performance have in the given context? This is much more
difficult than analyzing the relationship between traffic signs
and traffic for two reasons. (1) The second part of the link,
that-which-is-signified, is precisely the murkiest aspect of
our understanding of ritual. Not only are there numerous conflicting scholarly interpretations of the "meaning" or significance of particular rituals, but as already noted, there frequently is no single naive believers' notion of what the ritual
"means." (2) Street signs, duck tails, and verbal signs may

all, in principle, be translated or replaced by different signs
which serve the same purpose; the street sign could be replaced
by an announcement or by a traffic cop, duck tails could be replaced by other forms of information regarding the sexual characteristics of that particular duck,[20] words may be translated
by other words. Further, we can check whether or not there is
a good "translation" by noting the behavioral effects the new
sign has in the old situation.

It is not at all clear how one could "translate" one kind
of ritual behavior into an equivalent form. This is so, not
only because we are not sure how to measure any possible
changes in the situation under question, but also because we
have no, as yet, clear-cut, orderly way of designating "equivalent" forms of behavior.[21]

These considerations suggest that, while we tend to ascribe a communications role to ritual, it is not correct to
liken that role to (1) expressive or illustrative actions which
accompany and act out a particular myth or story, or (2) signs
or signifiers of a discrete or isolatable meaning. Leach[22] is
aware of these difficulties and he suggests that rituals are
related to myth in the way that deep grammar is related to discrete, articulated theories of grammar. He proposes that
Ritual : Myths :: Deep Grammar : Grammar Textbooks.

This is an attractive, if not very clear, proposition.
It would explain why there are so many different and incom-
patible native and scholarly theories of ritual. These theories
of ritual repeat the mistake of the older theories of grammar,
namely, they attempt to explain grammatical rules in semantic
terms. Leach also, metaphorically, describes rituals as
"carrier waves." While this changes the metaphor rather drastically (leaping from linguistics to radio-electronics), it
rightly emphasizes the point that, while rituals in themselves
may not be univocal information-bearing phenomena, they may
provide both raw material and structuralizing capabilities for
particular information-bearing sequences (meaningful actions).

To carry out his proposition a bit further, Leach is suggesting that we may be able to isolate "ritemes" similarly to
the way in which linguistics can isolate phonemes, morphemes,

etc., which are the constituent units of all languages. Thus,
once we had factored out the set of ritemes prevalent in a particular context (say a homogeneous culture group), we would
then be able to examine any full-bodied ritual in that culture
and systematically explain the significance of its constituent
parts and the organization as a whole.[23]

Leach also suggests rituals may be a language, code,
grammar, or syntax.[24] While these suggestions are obviously
tentative and exploratory, they do, I think, raise a number of
questions about the origins or physiological and developmental
bases of ritual behavior.

> (1) Can we construct a developmental hierarchy of
> behavior in which we could place rituals? For
> example: Unconditioned Response; Instincts; Innate
> Releasing Mechanism; Ritual (?); Conditioned Reflex;
> Operant Conditioning; "Advanced" Learning.

By placing "ritual" between innate releasing mechanisms[25] and
conditioned reflex, I am following these authors' suggestion
that rituals are indeed learned responses. But both their
sequence and their patterning suggest they rest on a non-
learned substrate. In a simple case, we can see this occur
when normal, day-to-day activities are ritualized, e.g., break-
ing bread with a friend may be a ritual as well as lunch. The
simplicity of this example does not carry over to what seem to
be more complex rituals, such as naming ceremonies, that have
no obvious biological or physiological base. Of course social
psychologists, anthropologists, and sociologists proffer rather
persuasive explanations of this "social" ritual, e.g., naming
ceremonies are parts of various rites of transition which the
society requires in order to maintain conceptual and emotional
control over the behaviors of its members. This could certainly be correct, but such explanations do not immediately
indicate how we are to understand the individual origins of
such complex ritual behaviors. To answer this question, one
would need to know a great deal about the biological and psychological bases of social "needs."

(2) Are there particular symbols which, because of
the structure of the human body and the nature of
human thought, we may call natural symbols?

For example, Brilliant concludes his study on gesture in
Roman art with an appendix devoted to tracing the development
of Roman law and court gestures from the Latin word, *manus*.

...*manus* meaning "hand," is used to describe that
significant appendage of the human body, which together with speech, above all distinguishes mankind
from the beasts....Behind all these usages [of the
term *manus*] lies the element of force, given or
received, which is fundamental to the symbolic
character of the hand.[26]

Brilliant's analysis follows a chronological line of development of the concept through Latin literature. Such a
genetic orientation is, of course, at the heart of the psychoanalytic model of the development of communication and psychoanalytic explanations in general. If we could combine, then,
the historical analysis Brilliant exemplifies with the psychoanalytic emphasis upon phylogenetic and ontogenetic development, we would then be able to ask the following questions of
any particular ritual behavior.

Upon what physiological substrate is the ritual based?
What are the species-specific behaviors which employ
those substrates?
How and with what associated experiences have these
species-specific behaviors been realized in the
developmental history of the individual?

While it would be interesting to scramble through the
psychoanalytic literature[27] and try to answer the various
questions I have raised about energy transformations and
physiological substrates of ritual behavior, I do not believe
there is sufficient clarity about the more fundamental metapsychological concepts that would constitute such high-level
answers to justify such a constructive endeavor. Consequently,
I propose to carry out the more modest tasks of first isolating
those more basic concepts and then evaluating their ability to
comprehend and possibly answer these higher level questions.

In the first half of this chapter, I have tried to show
two things: (1) that rituals have five salient characteristics

(they are human or animal, repetitive, functional, symbolic, and normative behaviors), and (2) that the general theory of psychoanalysis and particular metapsychological formulations of it seem relevant to many of the most basic questions and problems one may raise about the nature of ritual behavior (for example, about their energy bases, meaning, repetitiveness and genetic characteristics).

Play, Ritual, and Repetition Compulsion

It is not possible to clarify Freud's ideas on play and ritual without traversing the confusing and highly speculative terrain of the essay, *Beyond the Pleasure Principle*, itself. I will put the following questions to it.

Are adult rituals genetically related to infantile play?
Are infantile play and analogous adult rituals non-pathological?
Can play and ritual behaviors contribute to adaptation?

A first reading of the essay would indicate that the answer to each of these questions is yes. However, a second reading with special attention to the rhetorical aspects of the essay suggests that Freud's answer to the last two is no.

Beyond the Pleasure Principle

The crucial questions of the entire work is, What principle of mental functioning finally dominates the mental processes? Freud notes that it cannot be the pleasure principle since the majority of mental processes are not accompanied by psychic discharge, that is, pleasure.[28] Further, while we can say in many cases that the reality principle, which involves the postponement of discharge until suitable objects and environment are available, is a roundabout pleasure principle, there remains the very significant fact that there are "conflicts and dissensions that take place in the mental apparatus while the ego is passing through its development into more highly composite organizations."[29] Further, it turns out that the eventual expression of once pleasure-producing impulses (drive derivatives) creates a state of unpleasure for the ego.

> As a consequence of the old conflict which ended in
> repression, a new breach has occurred in the pleasure
> principle at the very time when certain instincts were
> endeavouring, in accordance with the principle, to
> obtain fresh pleasure.[30]

What would appear to be a major confusion in theory of
affects, that is, the theory of conscious emotional experiencing, leads Freud to the remarkable conclusion: "...there is no
doubt that all neurotic unpleasure is of that kind--pleasure
that cannot be felt as such."[31]

The apparent contradiction Freud so clearly utters here
can be explained by reference to his earliest remarks in the
"Project" in which he first stated many of the theorems re-
expressed in this chapter. In that earlier work he had had
similar conceptual difficulty when he tried to explain, via his
model of neuronic functioning, the mechanics of pleasure and
other affects (that is, the perception of qualities) in terms
of quantities (the activity of neural sets). This is no small
problem, for if we accept his judgment that neurotic unpleasure
is essentially "pleasure that cannot be felt as such," then a
science which hopes to explain and, through its application,
cure neuroses requires a noncontradictory theory of affects
(of pleasure and pain).

There are a number of ways out of this conceptual dilemma.
One way is to harken back to clinical theory and clinical experience which indicate that neurotic suffering has its roots
in frustrated desires for certain kinds of pleasure (e.g.,
incestuous union) that are forbidden. This observation, that
is, the recognition of such "unconscious" desires through
dreams, slips of tongue, and most of all, through the transference relationship, in conjunction with the tension-reduction
model of psychic functioning, allows us to conclude that neurotic symptoms are substitute formations and hence represent
indirect discharge of repressed wishes. Since pleasure is
theoretically defined as discharge,[32] it follows that neurotic
suffering is actually a certain kind of pleasure. However, as
Freud makes it clear in this initial chapter, the process by
which the ego is able to transform pleasure into nonpleasure
is obscured and yet is one of the central features of ego
development.[33]

A second way would be to grant to the ego-independent energies which, contrary to the nature and aim of the drives, do
not seek immediate discharge, but that are present in the
earliest phase of the ego as neutral energies which can enter
into conflict with instinctual upsurge and even countermand the
"pleasure principle" if the ego perceives the need for such
drastic action. This is essentially the route Freud takes in
the 1926 essay on anxiety and the ego. In that essay which,
of course, depends very much upon the 1923 essay, *The Ego and
the Id*, Freud grants a degree of autonomy from instinctual and
environmental forces to the ego which he does not in *Beyond the
Pleasure Principle*.

A third way to explain the fact of painful neurotic repetition is to remain faithful to the main features of instinct
theory and hence to look for another drive or principle of mental functioning which underlies the neurotic's compulsion to
repeat even the most painful of experiences. This is the way
Freud took in *Beyond the Pleasure Principle*.

In order to clarify the way in which Freud pursued this
third course, I will critically review each of the essay's
chapters and try to show how much of the obscurity and awkward-
ness of Freud's argument stem from the fact that he attempts
to explain the central phenomenon, the nature of the ego's
reaction to internal disruption, within the framework of the
libido theory, and in so doing literally drives the instinct
theory to death.

Chapter II

Freud discusses two kinds of painful repetition, children's
play which repeats painful experiences, and dreams that repeat
traumatic episodes in the dreamer's life. He first examines
the nature of repetition in traumatic neurosis. He makes the
interesting points that, "...a wound or injury inflicted simultaneously works as a rule *against* the development of neurosis,"[34]
and, "There is something about anxiety that protects its subject
against fright and so against fright-neurosis."[35] We may put
these facts in tabular form.

                              produces

mechanical trauma + fright	traumatic neurosis (anxiety dreams)
war experiences + fright	war neurosis (anxiety dreams)
war experiences + fright + wound	no neurosis
war experiences + anxiety	no neurosis

Freud says that these facts and especially the fact that the
victims of traumatic neurosis constantly dream about their
experiences "...astonishes people far too little."[36] Obviously
the simple wish-fulfillment theory of dreaming first proposed
in 1900 does not adequately account for recurring painful dreams.

Freud then examines another kind of repetition of painful
experiences. He describes a puzzling activity he observed an
eighteen-month-old child performing.

> This good little boy...had an occasional disturbing
> habit of taking any small objects he could get hold
> of and throwing them away from him into a corner,
> under the bed, and so on, so that hunting for his
> toys and picking them up was often quite a business.
> As he did this he gave vent to a loud, long-drawn-out
> "o-o-o-o," accompanied by an expression of interest
> and satisfaction. His mother and the writer of the
> present account were agreed in thinking that this
> was not a mere interjection but represented the
> German word *"fort"* [gone]. I eventually realized
> that it was a game....[37]

Freud analyzes the boy's game and suggests that it represents
the boy's attempt to symbolically repeat the experience of
losing his mother, who is *fort* too often for his likes, and
hence whom he may wish to punish by throwing out objects symbolically attached to her, just as Freud suggested Goethe had
done with reference to his parents.[38] As was the case with
traumatic neurosis, Freud notes that we cannot easily explain
this child's behavior in simple hedonistic terms; "The child
cannot possibly have felt his mother's departure as something
agreeable or even indifferent."[39] Can we say then that this
little boy's game represents behaviors which are not manifestations of and hence not explained by the pleasure principle?

Freud holds fire and looks for more orthodox explanations
within the purview of the pleasure principle. For example, we
might explain the child's action by noting that he may have
revenged himself on his mother, that is, gained discharge of

aggressive feelings, and so received a kind of pleasure.
Further, children frequently gain the pleasure of fantasy wish
fulfillment when, fulfilling their constant wish to be like
grown-ups, they duplicate the actions of grown-ups--even if
that action was painful to them. So, Freud concludes, such
cases give no evidence of "the operation of tendencies *beyond*
the pleasure principle, that is, of tendencies more primitive
than it and independent of it."[40]

Chapter III

Here Freud examines another example of the repetition of
painful events, those which occur in intense periods of the
transference neurosis, and he concludes that such examples,
and certain life histories of people who seem to passively
suffer a repeated unhappy fate, give him "courage to assume
that there really does exist in the mind a compulsion to repeat
which overrides the pleasure principle."[41]

In his discussion of transference neurosis, Freud distinguishes between the repetition of infantile wishes which, at
one time, would have yielded pleasure if fulfilled, and the
repetition of "unwanted situations and painful emotions"[42]
which had never been pleasurable.

> ...no lesson has been learnt from the old experience
> of these activities having led instead only to un-
> pleasure. In spite of that, they are repeated,
> under pressure of a compulsion.[43]

He notes that we can see an intimate merger between the
compulsion to repeat and the pleasure principle in children's
games. Also we can see that a therapist and his client struggle to bring the compulsion to repeat to their respective
sides.[44]

He concludes with the suggestive but quite unclear remarks
that such examples support the notion that there is something
more primitive, elementary, and "more instinctual [*triebhaft*]
than the pleasure principle which it over-rides."[45] These
dramatic descriptions of the compulsion to repeat--in other
places Freud describes it as "demonic"[46]--prepare us for the
even more dramatic speculations that follow.

Chapter IV

Here Freud offers a rather roundabout explanation of the four facts of traumatic war neuroses listed above. He reaches back into the (then unpublished) theories of the "Project"[47] and constructs a model of mental functioning based on a highly speculative interpretation of neural functioning.

Briefly stated, Freud suggests that the mental organization (here named in terms of the perception-consciousness distinction) is a phylogenetically evolved mechanism situated at the boundary between "inside" and "outside" the organism that has the primary job of maintaining an equilibrium between the quantities of excitation (psychic energy) which impinge upon it from within and from without.

The organization of neural cells and processes that shields the organism from both the effects of excessive external stimulation (which is experienced as pain) and internal stimulation (the effects of instinctual upsurges) is also the seat of consciousness and corresponds, roughly, to the ego of the later essays.[48] However, Freud claims that the way in which the ego defends the organism against excessive internal stimuli must differ radically from the way it shields the organism against excessive external stimuli.

> Toward the inside there can be no such shield, the excitations in the deeper layers extend into the system directly and in undiminished amount, in so far as certain of their characteristics give rise to feelings in the pleasure-unpleasure series.[49]

As a result, the ego must adopt various ways of reducing the intensity of the stream of internal stimuli which threaten the organism with pain (i.e., excessive stimulation).

One way is to treat the internal threat as if it were from the external world, "so that it may be possible to bring the shield against stimuli into operation as a means of defence against them."[50] If this fails, the organism then effects every possible defensive maneuver.

> At the same time, the pleasure principle is for the moment put out of action. There is no longer the possibility of preventing the mental apparatus from being flooded with large amounts of stimulus, and

> another problem arises instead--the problem of
> mastering the amounts of stimulus which have broken
> in and of binding them, in the psychical sense, so
> that they can then be disposed of.[51]

It is on the basis of this very compact model of psychic functioning that Freud explains the astonishing facts of traumatic
neurosis and the way in which the pleasure principle is put out
of action in other situations as well. Since the need to master or bind excessive stimuli is prior to the drive to discharge
tension (and so experience pleasure) it follows that organisms
will attempt to bind excessive stimuli even when such attempts
increase psychic pain (*unlust*). We may now, following Freud,
explain why it was that the presence of physical pain or
anxiety in potentially traumatic situations, such as war, prevented the occurrence of traumatic neurosis, particularly the
repetition of painful dreams.

(1) Take the last two cases first: war experiences +
fright + wound; war experiences + anxiety. We note that the
presence of anxiety or a wound effectively prevents the occurrence of repetition neuroses. We may explain the prophylactic
effect of physical and mental suffering by supposing that the
ego attempts to counteract excessive breaches in the stimulus
barrier. When the organism suffers a physical wound or intense
anxiety about possible danger, we conclude that the psychic
mechanism reacts to both dangers by setting up an "anti-
cathexis on a grand scale."[52] While this reduces the effective
energy available for other physical tasks, it increases the
ego's store of neutralizing energy with which it may seal subsequent breaches. Once this has been accomplished, the pleasure principle can once more dominate mental life.

(2) Mechanical trauma + fright and war experiences +
fright. In situations that produce these conditions (e.g.,
railway accidents or emergencies in war conditions), the ego is
caught unawares and as a consequence it is not ready to fend
off the excessive amount of stimuli which impinge upon it and
which create the experience of "fright" (*Schreck*). Because it
is caught at such a low ebb, so to speak, the ego system must
expend a great deal of energy to absorb the inflow of excessive

stimuli and attempt to "bind" them.[53] And how does it do this?
It accomplishes this task by creating within the mental mechanisms the condition of anxiety (a kind of unpleasure) which, had
it been present originally, would have prevented the overwhelm-
ing experience of fright and hence the excessive breach in the
protective shield.

We can also explain the function of traumatic dreams that
clearly are not simple wish fulfillments.

> We may assume, rather, that dreams are here helping to
> carry out another task, which must be accomplished
> before the dominance of the pleasure principle can
> begin. These dreams are endeavouring to master the
> stimulus retrospectively, by developing the anxiety
> whose omission was the cause of the traumatic
> neurosis.[54]

In Chapter V, Freud goes on to demonstrate how many other
compulsive features of neurotic phenomena, including transference neuroses, come about.

> The fact that the cortical layer which receives
> stimuli is without any protective shield against
> excitations from within must have as its result that
> these later transmissions of stimulus have a pre-
> ponderance in economic importance and often occa-
> sion economic disturbances comparable with traumatic
> neurosis.[55]

In other words, we see in many neurotic conditions an economic
situation similar to that of traumatic neurosis such that the
task of binding excessive stimuli, that is, preventing disruption of the psychic mechanisms itself, takes priority over all
other tasks.

> A failure to effect this binding would provoke a
> disturbance analogous to traumatic neurosis; and
> only after this binding has been accomplished would
> it be possible for the dominance of the pleasure
> principle (and of its modification, the reality
> principle) to proceed unhindered. Till then the
> other task of the mental apparatus, the task of
> mastering or binding excitations, would have
> precedence--not, indeed, in *opposition* to the
> pleasure principle, but independently of it and
> to some extent in disregard of it.[56]

It is at this point that Freud launches into the supra-
clinical speculations for which this essay is so well known,

e.g., *"the aim of all life is death."*[57] It is also at this
point that I wish to distinguish between Freud's clinical-
theoretical contributions on the psychopathological nature of
ritualization and his philosophic, evolutionary speculations
about the nature of all mental life, including its adaptive,
nonadaptive, normal, and the psychopathological dimensions.

From Binding Stimuli to the Death Instinct

Up to the second page in Chapter V, Freud only characterizes these features of mental life which may be "beyond the
pleasure principle" as fundamental features of the (ego's) need
to bind excessive stimuli. This would appear to place these
"compulsions" in an adaptive, generally constructive relationship to the organism. However, Freud rather subtly undermines
this positive valuation when he notes:

> The manifestations of a compulsion to repeat...exhibit
> to a high degree an instinctual [*Triebhaft*] character,
> and, when the act in opposition to the pleasure prin-
> ciple, give the appearance of some daemonic [*dämonisch*]
> force at work.[58]

This is a very skillfully wrought sentence; Freud's reference
to the driveness, and even the strange, uncanny, feelings which
observation of repetition creates in the viewer's mind, directly suggests that we see a great, suprahuman, and dreadful power
working here in opposition to the benefit and pleasures of the
individual. He quickly adds to this dramatic description more
illustrations of the awesomeness of the compulsion to repeat.

> This same compulsion to repeat frequently meets us as
> an obstacle to our treatment when at the end of an
> analysis we try to induce the patient to detach him-
> self completely from his physician. It may be pre-
> sumed, too, that when people unfamiliar with analysis
> feel an obscure fear--a dread of rousing something
> that, so they feel, is better left sleeping--what
> they are afraid of at bottom is the emergence of this
> compulsion with its hint of possession by some
> "daemonic" power.[59]

And does Freud also feel that such "daemonic" powers are better
left sleeping? As a spokesman for the value of psychoanalytic
treatment and as the author of "The Uncanny,"[60] he would answer

in the negative. However, in the context of this essay, he
clearly answers in the affirmative for, as he tells us on the
same page, there *is* a kind of suprahuman tendency in all organic life to return to its earlier conditions.[61]

Thus those people who dread the revelations that might be
uncovered by psychoanalytic treatment are, at least to this
degree, correct; they might well find themselves in the grip of
some demonic force which is biological rather than psychological and which therefore may not be easily treated by psychological therapy.[62]

Given that all instincts, even the sex instincts,[63] are
manifestations of the tendency to return to an earlier state of
things, it follows that all organic striving is towards the
very earliest state of existence which is the state of inor-
ganic existence, that is, death.[64]

A Difficulty in Our Path

It is clear that within *Beyond the Pleasure Principle* we
can find what appear to be bona fide psychoanalytic theorems
about the nature of repetition in pathological and nonpathological cases, e.g., the child's game and traumatic neuroses.
If we accepted the strands of evidence and logic which Freud
offers in favor of the notion of a fundamental tendency to repeat which is primary to the pleasure principle, we could then
follow his example and say that ritual behaviors (that is, behaviors which are human, repetitive, functional, symbolic, and
normative) are ultimately expressions of the compulsion to repeat. But, as I suggested above, the central question of the
first part of the essay (Is there a tendency operating within
the mind which is "beyond" the dominance of the pleasure principle?) rests upon a basic confusion between the concept of
pleasure as (simply) discharge of psychic energy and pleasure
as positive affective experience. More importantly, the essay's
most significant conclusions and most profound speculations are
especially liable to rather severe and convincing criticisms by
analysts, philosophers, biologists, and theoreticians. I shall
discuss three.

Barros[65] carefully reviewed all of the metapsychological
essays and most of the secondary literature on the psychoanalytic concepts of energy transformations and energy displacement.
He was specifically interested in elucidating the nature of
equilibrium-seeking mechanisms posited by analytic metapsychology and he showed, I think, that the general theory does not
imply that the mind is a simple tension-reduction mechanism
which operates like a closed equilibrium system seeking minimal
energy levels. Rather, he suggests, the dominant analytic
model is that of an open-ended equilibrium system in which the
mental apparatus seeks to attain a level of balance between
internal and external forces, not a minimization of those
forces or the level of mental activity. Thus he criticizes
Freud's willingness to confuse the tendency of the mental mechanism to *attain* a relative level of equilibrium with a tendency
for it to *restore* the earliest, original, level of equilibrium
which is a state of non-life, that is, death.[66]

Schur systematically examined the status of the repetition
compulsion as a regulatory principle of mental functioning on
par with the pleasure and reality principles. He suggested
Freud incorrectly used clinical and anecdotal observations of
people who exhibited compulsions-to-repeat to construct the
extremely high level notion of a repetition-compulsion (*Wieder-
holungszwang*).[67] He criticizes most of Freud's formulations
of the repetition compulsion and suggests that the clinical
phenomena of compulsion to repeat can be better explained as
the results of particular ego defenses, especially undoing,
e.g., as that defense is used by obsessional neurotics who find
themselves repeating stupid, painful, or senseless actions.[68]

Ricoeur[69] also criticizes Freud's torturous logic in the
essay and he goes on to ask a question that Schur and Barros
did not, namely, why would Freud so overextend himself and his
own clinical theory in such an obvious way with so little support? Ricoeur's answer is, in part, that Freud's goals were
more philosophic than they were scientific and that the hints,
suggestions, and rhetoric which pervade the essay show that
Freud's ultimate intention is to

...accustom us to see death as a figure of necessity,
to help us submit "to a remorseless law of nature, to
the sublime Ἀνάγκη" [Freud, *Beyond the Pleasure
Principle*, 45]; but above all to enable us to sing
the paean of life, of libido, of Eros![70]

If one sides with those who reject the main conclusions of
Beyond the Pleasure Principle, one is left to puzzle over the
ransacked edifice and search among its firmer foundations for
more useful materials. Thus our difficulty in accepting the
essay's main conclusions turns into an opportunity to reexamine
its contents. When we do this it seems to me that the essay's
most significant and most mysterious passages are those in
which Freud describes the little boy's game.

The Work of Mourning and the Work of Ritualization

I suggested above that a close reading of the essay would
indicate that the answer to the following questions is negative.

Are infantile play and analogous adult rituals nonpathological?
Can play and ritual behavior contribute to adaptation?

In his discussion of the little boy's game, Freud appears to
examine and then drop the possible interpretation that the
repetitive, painful qualities of the child's behavior indicate
the operation of tendencies beyond the pleasure principle. And
since the game evidently helped the child cope with the exigencies of his mother's frequent absence it would seem that
this kind of play (and by extension, adult rituals) can positively contribute to adaptation.

But what Freud implies in the main text he seems to deny
in the footnote which immediately follows this particular example. In the text Freud suggests that by throwing away the
object which was associated with his mother the child gained a
kind of revenge for the pain she caused him. In support of
this rather sinister portrait of the child's mind, he adds that
this same little boy was not displeased by his father's absence;
"...on the contrary he made it quite clear that he had no desire
to be disturbed in his sole possession of his mother."[71]

He then appends this footnote:

When this child was five and three-quarters, his
mother died. Now that she was really "gone"
("O-O-O"), the little boy showed no signs of grief.
It is true that in the interval a second child had
been born and had roused him to violent jealousy.[72]

I think this is a remarkably suggestive denouement to the seemingly innocent portrait Freud initiated with the neutral comments that the child's game was puzzling. For there is something uncanny about this seemingly innocent child and his game.
Although Freud maintains his neutral, descriptive tone, we cannot help but wonder at the nearly automatic viciousness which
he attributes to the boy and his feelings toward his father.
Obviously Freud means us to see that the boy's lack of regret
over his father's absence is typical of male children during
the oedipal period. One could find dozens of similar examples
in other Freud texts which explain that such aggression is the
result of the boy's love for his mother and fear of his father's
retaliation.[73]

In these earlier texts the boy's oedipal aggression toward
his father is a secondary function of his more primary erotic
impulses toward his mother. But when we read that this same
child did not grieve the loss of his mother either, the person
whom we would expect him to miss most, we are more willing to
wonder if indeed there is not some factor operating in him
which is more archaic or more fundamental than positive oedipal
desires.

Freud does not immediately draw that conclusion for us,
but it is clear from the second sentence in the footnote quoted
above that he is thinking along that line and yet he hastens to
add, lest he be too quickly criticized, that indeed there were
typical object-related disappointments in the child's relationship with his mother which might account for his lack of grief.
It is only in the last half of the essay that Freud will attempt
to show how very closely the compulsion to repeat is tied to
death and the individual's impulses to destructiveness.

However, rather than follow Freud as he develops the notion of the interdependence of repetition, destructiveness, and

death,[74] I should like to retreat and ask a question on which
the text is mute, namely, is there a relationship between the
child's game in which he "practices" losing an object and his
emotionless reaction to the real loss of his mother? Freud is
exasperatingly laconic on this rather central fact in the case
history; we do not know how the child responded to other people
after his mother's death, nor do we know if that seemingly
massive object loss figured in the development of a later neurosis. Unless we are willing to interpret the boy's ritual and
his lack of sorrow as expressions of his own aggressiveness
(derived from and a function of the death instinct), we can
only speculate about the relationship between his game and his
surprising heartlessness.

Perhaps the most obvious explanation of the child's lack
of grief is to assume that he had already worked through the
loss of his mother when, as Freud informs us, he became extremely jealous of the affection and attention she gave her
second child. And would not such working through be analogous
to the process of mourning which is extremely painful to the
ego?[75]

Yes, but we do not know how much working through occurred
after the arrival of the sibling. Yet we do know that even
before that event the boy played that puzzling, apparently
innocent game of *fort* in which he repeatedly inflicted upon
himself and suffered the symbolic loss of his beloved mother.

While there are numerous similarities in the way Freud
discusses the central notion of repetition in the two essays
which offer grounds for a more extensive comparison between
them, there are also enormous differences in their theoretical
superstructures. The most significant is that, while "Mourning
and Melancholia" marks the apex of the papers on metapsychology
which are predominantly concerned with elucidating the drive
theories of that period, *Beyond the Pleasure Principle* marks
the beginning of the last phase in Freud's thinking in which he
recast many of those earlier drive theories and introduced the
revolutionary concepts of ego, id, and superego. Therefore, in
order to more systematically answer the questions I raised
about adaptation and ritualization and the work of mourning and

the work of ritual, I propose to review the status and inter-
relationship of what seem to be the most central metapsychological concepts relevant to the neutral definition of ritual
elaborated in the first half of this chapter.

That definition was: ritual is human or animal activity
which is repetitive, functional, symbolic, and normative. The
boy's game was just such activity; it was repeated so frequently that Freud considered it puzzling; it seems to have reduced
the boy's terror at losing his mother; it involved, Freud says,
symbolic representations; and it was normative in that the
child seemed to attach a special importance to it. And, if we
accept Freud's initial interpretation, it served to regulate
the boy's relationship and perhaps need for his mother's actual
presence.

I suggest that the following five, low-level clinical concepts are both most central to Freud's interpretation of the
game and most compatible with our neutral definition of ritual.

Psychic Pain

This fundamental, phenomenological category is central to
all of Freud's thinking about the neuroses and by extension it
appears, as we have seen, in the metacultural essays in which
he explains that religion has the role of soothing every kind
of psychic pain, including object loss, oedipal defeats, narcissistic wounds, and the fear of death.

Pleasure-Unpleasure Principle

While, as we shall see below, Freud often elevated this
principle to the level of a general explanatory principle of
mental functioning, it is essentially a low-level clinical concept designed to account for the most obvious hedonistic features of human behavior, including ritual behavior.

Primary and Secondary Defense

Again, while Freud greatly expanded the theoretic aspects
of the concept of defense as he developed the metapsychology,
it originally served to classify peculiar forms of behavior
(e.g., hysteric attacks) which seemed to have the function of
protecting the patient from an unknown danger just as the boy's
game protected him.

Repetition (Hallucination and Restitution)

Both "hallucination" and "restitution" entail the notion
of repetition whether of an apparently nonpathological game or
religious ritual or of quite pathological and painful neurotic
symptoms. In suggesting that the child's game allowed him to
achieve a degree of mastery over a painful reality which he
could not otherwise effect, Freud allows us to infer that there
was something in the act of repetition itself which mimicked
that reality. From the child's point of view, such re-enactment
would be very similar to a kind of hallucination. From an outsider's point of view, the boy's game might appear, as it did
to Freud, to be a kind of symbolic restitution and "working
through." Indeed, immediately after describing the little
boy's game, Freud notes that children's games are very similar
to artistic production and aesthetic experiences which may also
be concerned with painful topics.

> Nevertheless, it emerges from this discussion that
> there is no need to assume the existence of a special
> imitative instinct in order to provide a motive for
> play...a reminder may be added that the artistic
> play and artistic imitation carried out by adults,
> which, unlike children's, are aimed at an audience,
> do not spare the spectators (for instance, in
> tragedy) the most painful experiences and can yet
> be felt by them as highly enjoyable.[76]

Inner and Outer Reality

These two concepts are based on a fundamental phenomenological distinction between self-as-experienced and others-as-
experienced. They are also basic to fundamental analytic notions, such as internalization, which represent attempts to
conceptualize these two types of psychological experiences.
Psychoanalytic theory is essentially a set of propositions
about the relationships between the inner world (of the intrapsychic self) and the outer world (all that is not part of
self, including, at times, one's own body or one's own thinking). Thus a psychoanalytic theory of ritual should include a
detailed examination of the way in which ritual behaviors affect the often shifting boundary that separates the inner world
from the outer world.

In order to construct such a theory, however, we must first review the geneology of each of these five concepts in the larger context of the development of Freud's thought. As Hartmann noted some thirty years ago, in order to comprehend the full value and meaning of psychoanalytic formulations one must understand their conceptual evolution. Therefore I propose to examine these five concepts as they emerge in the following periods of Freud's work, grouped according to their chronological and theoretic similarities.[77]

Period I--Pre-psychoanalytic writings, letters to Fliess,[78] and the "Project"

Period II--The Interpretation of Dreams

Period III--Papers on Metapsychology

Period IV--Papers on Ego Psychology

CHAPTER III

[1]Ten years ago this task would have been much more difficult than it is now. There has been a great deal of systematic
review and scholarly criticism done since that time on the
major features and concepts in Freud's entire corpus. Of primary importance to the Freud student is the Index volume to the
Standard Edition published in 1974 (vol. 24). With that volume
it is possible to rapidly review the use and development of all
major terms in Freud's texts. In addition, I have relied upon
the following authors' historical and textual works on psychoanalytic theory: Peter Amacher, *Freud's Neurological Education
and Its Influence on Psychoanalytic Theory*, Psychological
Issues 16 (New York: International Universities Press,
1965); H. Ellenberger, *The Discovery of the Unconscious* (New
York: Basic Books, 1970); E. Kris, Introduction to *The Origins
of Psycho-Analysis, Letters to Wilhelm Fliess, Drafts and Notes:
1887-1902* (ed. M. Bonaparte, A. Freud and E. Kris; trans. E.
Mosbacher and J. Strachey; New York: Basic Books, 1954); R.
Holt, "Freud's Mechanistic and Humanistic Images of Man," *Psychoanalysis and Contemporary Science* 1 (1972) 3-24; H. Nagera,
ed., *Basic Psychoanalytic Concepts of the Libido Theory*, Hampstead Clinic Psychoanalytic Library, vol. 1 (New York: Basic
Books, 1969); idem, *Basic Psychoanalytic Concepts on Metapsychology, Conflicts, Anxiety and Other Subjects*, Hampstead
Clinic Psychoanalytic Library, vol. 4 (New York: Basic Books,
1970); idem, *Basic Psychoanalytic Concepts on the Theory of Instincts*, Hampstead Clinic Psychoanalytic Library, vol. 3 (New
York: Basic Books, 1971); K. Pribram, "Freud's Project: An Open,
Biologically Based Model of Psychoanalysis," pp. 81-92 in *Psychoanalysis and Current Biological Thought* (ed. N. Greenfield
and W. Lewis; Madison: University of Wisconsin, 1965); D. Shakow
and D. Rapaport, *The Influence of Freud on American Psychology*
(New York: International Universities Press, 1964). Finally, I
have consulted the following texts which review particular metapsychological concepts: M. Gill, *Topography and Systems in Psychoanalytic Theory*, Psychological Issues 10 (New York: International Universities Press, 1963) on the topographic theory;
R. Holt, "A Critical Examination of Freud's Concept of Bound
vs. Free Cathexis," *Journal of the American Psychoanalytic
Association* 10 (1962) 475-525, on free and bound energy; idem,
"A Review of Some of Freud's Biological Assumptions and Their
Influence on His Theories," pp. 93-124 in *Psychoanalysis and
Current Biological Thought*; D. Rapaport, "Some Metapsycho-
logical Considerations Concerning Activity and Passivity," pp.
530-568 in *The Collected Papers of David Rapaport* (ed. M. Gill;
New York: Basic Books, 1967); idem, "The Theory of Ego Autonomy:
A Generalization," pp. 722-744 in *The Collected Papers of David
Rapaport*; idem, "On the Psychoanalytic Theory of Motivation,"
pp. 853-916 in *The Collected Papers of David Rapaport*; idem, *The
Structure of Psychoanalytic Theory*, Psychological Issues 6
(New York: International Universities Press, 1960); R. Schafer,

Aspects of Internalization (New York: International Universities Press, 1968); M. Schur, *The Id and the Regulatory Principles of Mental Functioning* (New York: International Universities Press, 1966).

[2]Quoted in E. R. Leach, "Ritual," p. 521 in *International Encyclopedia of the Social Sciences* 13 (ed. D. L. Sils; New York: Macmillan, 1968).

[3]Ruth Benedict, "Ritual," pp. 396-398 in *Encyclopaedia of the Social Sciences* 13 (New York: Macmillan, 1934); E. Erikson, "The Ontogeny of Ritualization," in *Psychoanalysis--A General Psychology* (ed. Loewenstein et al.; New York: International Universities Press, 1966); Leach, "Ritual"; H. Mol, "The Sacralization of Identity" (typewritten, 1975), published as *Identity and the Sacred* (Oxford: Blackwell, 1976; New York: Free Press, 1976).

[4]Benedict, "Ritual," 397.

[5]S. Lukes, "Political Ritual and Social Integration," *Sociology* 9/2 (1975) 291.

[6]Talcott Parsons, *The Structure of Social Action* (Glencoe: Free Press, 1949).

[7]Dan Sperber, *Le Symbolisme en Général* (Paris: Hermann, 1964).

[8]Jane Harrison, *Ancient Art and Ritual* (London: Williams and Norgate, 1913).

[9]Leach, "Ritual."

[10]For example, the keystone in a Roman arch is designed to remain quite fixed all the while it performs the important function of resisting the forces exerted by its neighboring stones.

[11]Freud, "Obsessive Actions and Religious Practices," and "Notes upon a Case of Obsessional Neurosis"; J. S. Huxley, "The Courtship-Habits of the Great Crested Grebe (podiceps cristatus); with an Addition to the Theory of Sexual Selection," *Proceedings of the Zoological Society of London* 35 (1914) 491-562; Peter Berger, *The Sacred Canopy: Elements of a Sociological Theory of Religion* (New York: Doubleday, 1967) 40-41.

[12]Rapaport, *Structure of Psychoanalytic Theory*, 90-100.

[13]S. Lukes, "Some Problems About Rationality," pp. 194-213 in *Rationality* (ed. Brian Wilson; New York: Harper and Row, 1970); idem, "Political Ritual"; Leach, "Ritual"; M. Hollis, "Reason and Ritual," pp. 221-239 in *Rationality*.

[14]Freud, *Interpretation of Dreams*, chap. VII; "The Theory of Symbolism," *British Journal of Psycho-Analysis* 9 (1916) 181 and in *Papers on Psychoanalysis* (5th ed.; London: Bailliere, Tindall and Cox, 1948) 87-144.

[15]Freud, "Obsessive Actions and Religious Practices";
idem, "A Mythological Parallel to a Visual Obsession," *SE* 14
(1957 [1916b]) 337-338; idem, "Medusa's Head," *SE* 18 (1955
[1940c]) 273-274.

[16]Jones, "Theory of Symbolism," 116.

[17]Ricoeur, *Freud and Philosophy*, 502-505.

[18]Ricoeur's analysis is, of course, much more extensive
than this remark indicates. In particular, he raises the very
important question of how we are to understand the process by
which the nonsymbolic (e.g., sexual) impulse is raised to the
level of symbol (ibid., 502).

[19]Konrad Lorenz, *On Aggression* (London: Methuen, 1966).

[20]But Lorenz notes that for some species there is only one
sign which carries the appropriate information, the absence of
which can lead to uncontrolled aggression or inhibit all sexual
contact (ibid.).

[21]But Roy L. Birdwhistell (*Introduction to Kinesics: (An
Annotation System for Analysis of Body Motion and Gesture)*
[Louisville: University of Louisville, 1952]) might prove to be
very helpful. Also see M. Davis, *Understanding Body Movement:
An Annotated Bibliography* (New York: Arno, 1972).

[22]Leach, "Ritual."

[23]But, as Leach remarks, this would be no easy task (e.g.,
often that person "raised on high" bears the most status in a
particular group), yet a frequent motif of very high status for
kings is that they may remain seated while all others stand
(ibid., 523-524).

[24]Ibid., 523-525.

[25]See Lorenz, *On Aggression*; Erikson, "Ontogeny of
Ritualization"; René A. Spitz, *No and Yes: On the Genesis of
Human Communication* (New York: International Universities
Press, 1957); idem, "Aggression and Adaptation," *Journal of
Nervous and Mental Diseases* 149 (1969) 81-90.

[26]R. Brilliant, *Gesture and Rank in Roman Art*, Memoirs of
the Connecticut Academy of Arts and Sciences 14 (New Haven:
The Academy, 1963) 215.

[27]For example, the above remarks on the semantic-
grammatical nature of ritual suggest that classical hysteria
might be a better psychiatric analogy of normal ritual than
obsessional neurosis. That is, the crucial features of hysteria, as described by Breuer and Freud in 1895, are remarkably
similar to the five features of ritual behavior described above;
see Breuer and Freud, *Studies on Hysteria*, *SE* 2 (1955 [1895d])
parts III and IV.

[28]See Rapaport's lecture notes on the meaning of the term "pleasure." Freud often gets into trouble when he confuses the metapsychological definition of pleasure: "discharge" with the experiential "feelings of pleasure"; Schur makes the same point (*The Id*, 125-128).

[29]Freud, *Beyond the Pleasure Principle*, 10.

[30]Ibid., 11.

[31]Ibid.

[32]Ibid., 8.

[33]Ibid., 10.

[34]Ibid., 12.

[35]Ibid., 13.

[36]Ibid.

[37]Ibid., 14-15.

[38]Sigmund Freud, "A Childhood Recollection from *Dichtung und Wahrheit*," *SE* 17 (1955 [1917b]) 147-172.

[39]Idem, *Beyond the Pleasure Principle*, 15.

[40]Ibid., 17.

[41]Ibid., 22.

[42]Ibid., 21.

[43]Ibid.

[44]Ibid., 23.

[45]Ibid.

[46]Ibid., 35.

[47]Sigmund Freud, "A Project for a Scientific Psychology," *SE* 1 (1966 [1950a]) 175-342.

[48]Idem, *The Ego and the Id*, *SE* 19 (1961 [1923b]) 3-66, and *Inhibitions, Symptoms and Anxiety*, *SE* 20 (1959 [1926d]) 77-174.

[49]Idem, *Beyond the Pleasure Principle*, 29.

[50]Ibid.

[51]Ibid., 29-30.

[52]Ibid., 30.

[53] Ibid., 30-31.

[54] Ibid., 32.

[55] Ibid., 34.

[56] Ibid., 35.

[57] Ibid., 38.

[58] Ibid., 35; *GW* 13.36.

[59] Freud, *Beyond the Pleasure Principle*, 36.

[60] Idem, "The Uncanny," *SE* 17 (1955 [1919h]) 219-256.

[61] Idem, *Beyond the Pleasure Principle*, 36.

[62] Ibid., 37-40.

[63] In the sense that the impulse to conjugate might, Freud speculates, be the result of a kind of archaic splitting of a bisexual unity which, as Plato described in the Symposium, present-day homisexuals strive to repair by copulating. However, in a grander sense the sex instincts are unique for by seeking to conjugate they manifest the more fundamental instinct of Eros which is the great antagonist to Ananke. Ricoeur notes (*Freud and Philosophy*, 291): "If the living substance goes to death by an inner movement, what fights against death is not something internal to life, but the conjugation of two mortal substances. Freud calls this conjugation Eros...it is always with another that the living substance fights against its own death...."

[64] Freud, *Beyond the Pleasure Principle*, 38.

[65] Carlos P. Barros, "Thermodynamic and Evolutionary Concepts in the Formal Structure of Freud's Metapsychology," pp. 72-111 in *World Biennial of Psychiatry and Psychotherapy* (ed. Silvano Arieti; New York: Basic Books, 1973).

[66] Ibid., 101.

[67] Schur, *The Id*, 159, n. 5.

[68] Ibid., 153-193.

[69] Ricoeur, *Freud and Philosophy*.

[70] Ibid., 290-291.

[71] Freud, *Beyond the Pleasure Principle*, 16.

[72] Ibid., 16, n. 1.

[73] Freud, *Interpretation of Dreams*, 261-266.

[74]But see Ricoeur, *Freud and Philosophy*, 294-296.

[75]Sigmund Freud, "Mourning and Melancholia," *SE* 14
(1957 [1917e]) 239-258.

[76]Idem, *Beyond the Pleasure Principle*, 17.

[77]Obviously, this division is schematic and done for the
sake of clarity in our discussion. For a similar treatment,
see Philip S. Holzman, *Psychoanalysis and Psychopathology* (New
York: McGraw Hill, 1970).

[78]Since vol. 1 of the *Standard Edition* has the better text
of the "Project" and the *Origins of Psycho-Analysis* has a more
complete set of letters to Fliess, I will use the former in
discussing the "Project" and the latter as a resource for the
letters.

CHAPTER IV

THE FIRST PERIOD--PRE-PSYCHOANALYTIC WRITINGS
AND THE "PROJECT"

The pre-history of psychoanalysis has been extremely well
researched and the sources, personalities, and opinions (both
scientific and philosophic) which influenced Freud have been
carefully investigated. In addition, many able and psycho-
analytically knowledgeable scholars have assessed the logic,
rigor, and influence, for ill or good, of the "Project." I do
not intend to duplicate their labors. Rather, by leaning on
their findings I believe we can quickly get to the core theories and models of mental functioning which Freud produced in
this first period.

As I suggested above and shall try to demonstrate below,
a great deal of the complexity of Freud's concepts and the
theories into which he incorporates them stems from the fact
that he almost always, except perhaps in the very speculative
chapters of the later works, attempts to maintain allegiance
both to observational data adduced in his own work with patients and to the rather narrow principles of the reductionistic philosophy of science he absorbed in his training with
Brücke.[1] When he finds that the particular explanation or
model he labors over cannot account for a particular observation, he quite willingly abandons it and searches for an alternate explanation. This leads us to admire his honesty but rue
the confusion which often results when he reintroduces the
formerly forsaken model or concept in a later section where it
might carry out his original project a bit further. Our confusion is increased when, as in the case of the central concept
"cathexis" (*Besetzung*), he uses very high-level terms derived
from the physiological model with little or no theoretical
discussion of their psychological meaning. Therefore, it may
be helpful to distinguish the particular set of principles and
criteria with which Freud constructed his theories of hysteria
and the other neuroses from the particular observations he made
of those diseases. In the first phase of his career, the explanatory model which dominates his theorizing is derived from

the physicalist school of Helmholtz and others;[2] the set of
data was primarily hysteria and obsessional neurosis.

The Physicalist Program

Bernfeld[3] and others have carefully documented the particular dominance that the views and philosophy of science of
Helmholtz and Brücke had upon nineteenth-century German psychology in general, and on Freud's early development as scien-
tist in particular. It was, according to the historians, a
period of great advances and great discoveries in neurology,
pathology, and anatomical studies. Freud himself participated,
under Brücke's stewardship, in significant research and, by his
middle thirties, had published major texts on infantile
neurology.

An obvious corollary of this commitment to a reductionistic philosophy of science is that one cannot accept as a complete explanation a theorem, a treatise, or a concept which
does not at least in principle refer to the most basic biological or chemical properties of matter. Given this point of
view, it is readily apparent to us, as it was to Freud, that a
truly scientific psychology would refer to or be founded upon
principles derived from the more basic sciences of biology and
neurology, just as these would be, in principle, founded upon
the even more basic sciences of physics and chemistry. It is
this point of view which clearly animated Breuer, Freud's col-
laborator in the 1892 and 1895 studies on hysteria, to propose
that one might best conceive of neural transmissions and structures as electrical mechanisms.

This is not to say that Freud and Breuer were unaware of
the many philosophic and technical difficulties inherent in the
position of an absolute reductionistic approach to psychical
phenomena. Freud wrote in his text *On Aphasia*: "The chain of
the physiological processes in the nervous system probably does
not stand in any causal relation to the psychical processes."[4]

However, as we shall see in the "Project" Freud attempted
to formulate explanations which would account for both types of
phenomena. An examination of that work, in conjunction with

the historical research mentioned above, allows us to list the
following assumptive principles which underlie all of Freud's
efforts to construct a physiological psychology.

(1) Psychological forces or energies are ultimately a
function of biological forces or energies, which in
turn are ultimately functions of physical and chemical
forces.

(2) Psychological experiences and psychological phenomena (e.g., dreams) are dependent upon and finally
functions of physiological-neurological processes.

(3) Mental states are ultimately brain or neural
states.

To these rather common, reductionistic principles, Freud
added the following assumptions that became explicit criteria
with which he formulated his own and judged other psychologies.

(4) Higher forms develop out of lower forms.

(5) Psychological processes obey the law of the conservation of energy and psychological systems tend to
divest themselves of energy (excitation).

(6) Reality, as it is defined in various ways, is
ultimately inhospitable and painful.

Because these last three assumptions are less obvious and
more complex than the first three, I will discuss each of them
in turn.

(4) This principle is a cornerstone of many of Freud's
psychological theories and all of his sociological explanations.
It forms the basis for the genetic point of view, i.e., that
contemporary behaviors, especially psychopathological ones, are,
finally, the products of earlier mishaps in the development of
the psychic apparatus.[5] It is central to Freud's analysis of
cultural evolution (e.g., *Totem and Taboo*) and his predictions
of cultural change (e.g., *The Future of an Illusion*).

By the time Freud was a young man, the principle that
higher forms develop out of lower forms had secured broad support in biology (Haeckel's law that ontogeny recapitulates
phylogeny), evolutionary theory (Darwin's picture of the des-
cent of man), and neurological theory (Jackson's neural integration model which stipulated that higher systems of neural
integration inhibit lower ones).[6]

In addition, a more or less complete allegiance to this
principle underlies the very central analytic notion of "regression" which dominates many of Freud's fundamental theories.[7]
By 1919, that is, by the end of the third period in the development of the metapsychology, the concept "regression" provided
one of the central threads for Freud's metapsychological as
well as metacultural speculations. In 1919 he appended the
following comments to the section on "regression" in Chapter
VII of *The Interpretation of Dreams.*

> Nor can we leave the subject of a regression in dreams
> without setting down in words a notion by which we
> have already repeatedly been struck and which will
> recur with fresh intensity when we have entered more
> deeply into the study of the psychoneuroses: namely
> that dreaming is on the whole an example of regres-
> sion to the dreamer's earliest condition, a revival
> of his childhood, of the instinctual impulses which
> dominated it and of the methods of expression which
> were then available to him. Behind this childhood
> of the individual we are promised a picture of a
> phylogenetic childhood--a picture of the development
> of the human race, of which the individual's devel-
> opment is in fact an abbreviated recapitulation
> influenced by the chance circumstances of life.

The first clause of this principle, that psychological
systems conserve energy, was based upon Helmholtz' reformula-
tion of the principle of the conservation of energy first described by Jules Robert Mayer in 1842.[8] As such it amounts to
a restatement of the first law of thermodynamics; that the sum
of actual and potential energies within a given system remains
constant in every case.

The second clause, that psychological systems tend to
divest themselves of energy, is based upon the second law of
thermodynamics, which was formulated by Lord Kelvin in 1850 and
Rudolph Clausius in 1851. In its most general form, this law
states that, in a closed system, there is a tendency for diver-
gent energy levels to reach equilibrium. In the language of
the early researchers, the second law states that heat will not
pass spontaneously from a body of low temperature to a body of
higher temperature.[9]

It is clear that Freud wanted to apply both laws to the
mental mechanism, and as we shall see in our analysis of the

"Project," he frequently attempts to explain psychological functioning in precisely this way. Indeed, as late as 1932, in his letter to Einstein on war, he suggests that physics remained the prototypical science and that his notion of Eros and destruction was analogous to the physical laws of attraction and repulsion.[10]

It was Freud's intermittent fidelity to the psychological version of the second law which accounts for one of the more inconsistent features of his formulations on psychic energy. That is, a strict application of the principle that the organism tends to divest itself of stimuli generates a model of a mental apparatus which has the primary function of tension reduction. However, as many authors noted then and many have noted since, this is much too simplistic an account of a mechanism which underlies the immense variety of stimuli-seeking behaviors that children, adults, and animals engage in. Both R. W. White, in his critique of Freud's economic theory of the ego,[11] and R. R. Holt, in his essay on Freud's biological model,[12] note that, by itself, this model and the high-level theories of the ego which Freud erected upon it, are simply inadequate to the actual phenomena.

However, a careful reading of even the earliest formulation suggests that Freud was aware of these explanatory inadequacies and, in fact, in the "Project" he very clearly recognizes that the mental mechanism, especially "the ego," is not a simple mechanism reflexively oriented toward discharge but that it actually increases the store of stimuli with which it may carry out complex tasks. In terms of the thermodynamic model, he conceives of the mind as an equilibrium-seeking mechanism which must operate as a system open to recurrent energization by both the drives (a source of internal stimuli) and reality (a source of external stimuli).[13]

The sixth assumption, that reality is painful and generally inhospitable, first appears in Freud's early attempts to account for the development of high-level, secondary process thinking, and what he called reality testing. It will be easier to clarify the compound meaning of the term "reality" and its particular painfulness by simply listing the variety of Freud's uses of that term.

(1) In terms of the simple thermodynamic model of the mental mechanism of reflexive discharge, and the definition of pain as heightened tension, it follows that that which increases stimulation (e.g., outer world) is painful.

(2) In terms of the thermodynamic equilibrium model of the mental mechanism, pain results from the nonbinding of energy/cathexis, that is, pain occurs when the ego is constantly cathected--neurones are not able to channel off excitation. Therefore that which cannot be psychically bound will be (potentially) painful. This is the key point in Freud's early definition of reality testing; reality refers to that source of excitations or impingements which are neither subject to the person's psychological control nor coincide with his wishes.[14]

This latter condition follows from Freud's fundamental hypotheses, first formulated in the "Project," that the infant only learns to distinguish between its own wishes (desires for pleasuring) and the outer, real world, when that world frustrates it. If frustration does not occur, Freud argues, the infant blissfully imagines that the breast which feeds it and the warm body that protects it are extensions of its own wishes. Thus, it follows that the infant-child will only come to know the reality of its mother when she fails to accurately fulfill its needs.

(3) In "Instincts and Their Vicissitudes," Freud used the pain-specific nature of reality to explain the origins of the distinction between inside and outside self.

> Let us imagine ourselves in the situation of an almost
> entirely helpless living organism, as yet unoriented
> in the world, which is receiving stimuli in its ner-
> vous substance. This organism will very soon be in
> a position to make a first distinction and first
> orientation. On the one hand, it will be aware of
> stimuli which can be avoided by muscular action
> (flight); these it ascribes to the external world.
> On the other hand, it will also be aware of stimuli
> against which such action is of no avail and whose
> character of constant pressure persists in spite of
> it; these stimuli are the signs of an internal
> world, the evidence of instinctual needs.[15]

In the great essay, "Mourning and Melancholia," Freud notes that having suffered the painful discovery of the separate reality of a significant other or ideal, at the death or absence of that person one must suffer another painful process, for

> reality testing has shown that the loved object no
> longer exists, and it proceeds to demand that all
> libido shall be withdrawn from its attachments to
> the object. This demand arouses understandable
> opposition....This opposition can be so intense that
> a turning away from reality takes place and a cling-
> ing to the object through the medium of a hallucina-
> tory wishful psychosis.[16]

(4) In a short essay, "Negation,"[17] Freud refers back to his earliest conditions of the infant's experience of the world and the way in which reality (understood as not-self) was differentiated.

> The function of judgement is concerned in the main
> with two sorts of decisions. It affirms or disaffirms
> the possession by a thing of a particular attribute;
> and it asserts or disputes that a presentation has
> an existence in reality. The attribute to be decided
> about may originally have been good or bad, useful
> or harmful. Expressed in the language of the oldest--
> the oral--instinctual impulses, the judgement is: "I
> should like to eat this," or "I should like to spit
> it out...." As I have shown elsewhere, the original
> pleasure-ego wants to introject into itself everything
> that is good and to eject from itself everything that
> is bad. What is bad, what is alien to the ego and
> what is external are, to begin with, identical.[18]

In the philosophical works, *The Future of an Illusion* and *Civilization and Its Discontents*,[19] Freud continually stresses that reality is more like the lifeless patterning of forces and particles which, as he had learned from Exner and others, is without quality but only quantities set in motion, than it is like the rosy pictures that religion and popular philosophies portray in their eternal illusions. Thus adherence to the scientific value of truthfulness reveals, according to Freud, the painful fact that reality is finally not as we would wish it. Rather, as Ricoeur notes, "This text [*The Future of an Illusion*] leaves no doubt; ...reality is the world shorn of God."[20]

"Project for a Scientific Psychology"

Freud made his first major statements on psychic pain and
the four other concepts in the "Project for a Scientific Psychology" of 1895. In that work he intended to place psychology
on a firm scientific basis by representing "psychical processes
as quantitatively determinate states of specifiable material
particles."[21] In the "Project," Freud puts forth a sustained
deductive argument which rests upon three premises: (1) that
the principle of inertia or the Law of the Conservation of
Energy discovered by Mayer in 1842 holds in all cases of psychical activity; (2) that psychical activity is a function of
psychic energy levels; and (3) that the neurones are the material particles which transmit that psychic energy.

The first premise is based upon clinical observation.
Freud found that patients suffering from "excessively intense"
ideas needed to rid themselves of an excessive internal excitation. This suggested the principle that psychic energy (like
electric or hydraulic energies) may be stored and at some later
time discharged. This also suggested to Freud that perhaps all
mental functioning required the storage and release of psychic
energy (premise two). Recent work in histology convinced him
that the neurones transmitted psychic energy (premise three).
Further, clinical features of hysteria seemed to show that the
neurones (assuming they are the material conductors of psychic
energy) tend to divest themselves of psychic impulse (hereafter "Q"); "On this basis the structure and development as
well as the functions (of neurones) are to be understood."[22]
Freud distinguished two kinds of Q: when (1) Q (as external
stimulus) impinges upon the organism it produces (2) Qh (internal excitation) within the organism.[23] This Qh is felt as tension and in primitive organisms it is discharged by the muscu-
lar mechanisms of flight or withdrawal or by any other pathway
which best facilitates total discharge.

However, in more complex organisms the nervous system receives Q from the somatic unit itself in the form of "drives"
or "somatic demands," e.g., hunger, sex, and respiration.
Since it cannot withdraw from these endogeneous stimuli, it
can reduce the tension or increase in Qh which results only by

satisfying the particular need with which it is associated.
In order to gain such satisfaction, the organism must (often)
make a sustained effort at dealing with its external and internal environments. Such sustained efforts require a pool or
store of psychic energy (Qh) from which the organism can draw
the necessary energy. This pooling of Qh forms the primitive
ego which has the task of coping with these internal demands
and exigencies in the external world. Thus, complex organisms
must bear a continuous tension, although they too, like all
organic life, strive to keep the Qh level as low as possible.

As mentioned above, Freud based much of his thinking in
the "Project" on then recent work in neurology and histology
which showed that the entire nervous system was composed of
"neurones" which were cells that received and conducted excitations through a central axis (the axion). So he concludes, "If
we combine this account of the neurones with the conception of
the Qh theory, we arrive at the idea of a *cathected* neurone
filled with a certain Qh, while at ohter times it may be
empty."[24] In terms of the primary tendency of organisms, discharge of external Q, the neurone would serve as a model for
the entire nervous system, a structure for ridding the organism
of tension. In terms of the secondary process, storage of internal Qh, a problem arises. If we assume the neurone to be
the functioning unit in the secondary processes as well as in
the first (and we do), then we must assume some means whereby
the neurones store Qh as well as discharge it.

Memory

Further, "a psychological theory deserving any consideration must furnish an explanation of 'memory.'"[25] Now memory
entails that there be a permanent alteration, a record, in
nervous tissue such that future excitations do not erase it.
Thus we must account for the complex organism's ability to remember (to store Qh) and to receive fresh stimuli without
altering the record of past excitations.

One way out of these problems is to assume there are two
classes of neurones: (1) those which allow Qh to pass through,
i.e., which do not have "contact barriers" that impede the flow

of Qh, and (2) those which have contact barriers that allow Qh
to pass only with difficulty. This second class of neurones
might then, after each excitation, be in an altered state and
so, acting like a casting of that excitation, represent memory.[26]
We may then speak of the first class of neurones, hereafter φ
neurones, as permeable and assume that they operate in perception. We may speak of the second class of neurones, hereafter
ψ neurones, as impermeable and assign to them the function of
memory "and of psychical processes in general."[27]

Learning

Reasoning back from the nature of memory and learning, we
must say of the ψ neurones that (1) they are permanently altered by the passage of an excitation, and (2) because skills
related to and relying upon memory processes can be developed,
this alteration must consist in the contact barriers of the
neurones becoming more permeable, i.e., like those of the φ
neurones; "We shall describe this state of the contact barriers
as their degree of *facilitation*."[28] We can say then that memory is represented by the facilitations existing between the
neurones. Further, since excitations appear to follow particular "associative" paths, there must be differences in facilitation among the entire set of ψ neurones else it would not "be
possible to see why one pathway should be preferred. We can
therefore say still more correctly that *memory is represented
by the differences in the facilitations between the ψ
neurones.*"[29]

Everyday experience tells us that intensity of memory depends upon the strength of the original impression and upon the
number of repetitions. We can explain this fact by the neurone
theory and say that facilitation depends upon the quantity of
Qh which passes through the ψ neurones in the excitatory process and upon the number of repetitions of that process. We
recall that the primary function of the nervous system was to
both perceive the organism's environment (the φ neurones serve
this function) and to discharge Qh arising from external Q.
Its secondary function was to store Qh so that the organism
might have a source of psychic energy with which it could meet

the exigencies of life. Yet the organism must avoid being
overly filled with this stored Qh. In order to maintain a
tolerable level of psychic tension, the organism sets up
facilitations within the ψ neurone system which act as discharge routes and so serve the primary function, i.e., ridding
the organism of excessive excitation.

The external world impinges upon the organism in very many
ways, so many that we might suspect there is some way by which
the organism is shielded from at least some of the external Q.
Examining the structure of the φ neurones,[30] we find that they
terminate in cellular structures which receive the exogeneous
stimuli first rather than on the surface. These cellular
structures might have the function of reducing the amount of Q
reaching the φ neurones and so allowing only *quotients* of Q to
reach them. In this structure we have a

> ...glimpse of a trend which may perhaps govern the
> construction of the nervous system out of several
> systems: an ever increasing keeping off of Qh from
> the neurones. Thus the structure of the nervous
> system would serve the purpose of *keeping off Qh* from
> the neurones and its function would serve the purpose
> of *discharging it.*[31]

Pain

All biological contrivances have limits beyond which they
fail in their specific function. Assuming the correctness of
the above description of the structure and function of the nervous system, it seems reasonable to conclude that a failure on
the part of the neurone systems would result in the experience
of pain.

> Everything that we know of pain fits in with this.
> The nervous system has the most decided inclination
> to a flight from pain. We see in this a manifesta-
> tion of the primary trend against a raising of Qh
> tension, and we infer that pain consists *in the
> irruption of large Q's into* ψ.[32]

We can now account for the observed fact that pain passes along
all possible discharge paths and ignores the contact barriers
of the ψ system. Because pain is the irruption of an excessive
number of Q's into the φ and ψ neurones, it is able to produce
its own facilitations and so cross usually impermeable barriers.

(Physical) pain produces in ψ neurones (1) a large rise in Qh which is experienced as unpleasure, (2) an inclination to discharge which may take different forms, and (3) a facilitation between the urge to discharge and the mnemic image of the object which excites the pain. Now if this mnemic image is recathected, for instance by a new perception of a similar object, a state arises which is like pain in that it is unpleasurable and demands discharge. It is unlike pain in that it does not involve perception; it constitutes *psychic* pain.

Since perception of a similar object is not sufficient to raise the Qh level to an unpleasurable level, we must assume that owing to the (postulated) process of re-cathexis the perception acts as an activation energy and releases Qh stored up in the soma, that is, it taps a store of endogenous Q. If this is so, then we must assume the existence of "key" neurones which store Qh and to which "the image of the hostile object has acquired an excellent facilitation."[33]

Pain, Quality, and Consciousness

Reflecting on the nature of pain, we realize, Freud says, that like pleasure it comprises a range of qualities and, that, in fact, all conscious experiencing is the experiencing of qualities,[34] "sensations which are *different* in a multiplicity of ways and whose *difference* is distinguished according to its relations with the external world."[35] Now, since, as already noted, science tells us that the external world is only one of quantitative fluctuations, it follows that qualities are functions of the psychic apparatus.

But on examining the two systems, φ and ψ, we see that neither could account for the experience of quality; φ neurones are too fundamental and basic to exemplify the high-level process of consciousness, and the ψ neurones seem primarily responsible for memory processes and "...this, speaking generally, is *without quality*. Remembering brings about *de norma* nothing that has the peculiar character of perceptual quality."[36] So Freud assumes that there must be a third neurone system, that he terms ω, which is responsible for conscious sensations of quality.

Because Freud adheres to his strict distinction between quantities and qualities, he must find some way of accounting for, within the mechanistic quantitative model so far erected, the passage and transmission of "qualities." But he cannot do this in terms of the simple Qh theory for assuming that the ω system lies behind the ψ system,[37] and that the tendency to reduce total quantity of excitation within the system persists, "it is to be suspected that the system is moved by still smaller quantities. It would seem as though the characteristic of quality (that is, conscious sensation) comes about only where quantities are so far as possible excluded."[38] Freud notes:

> At this point, however, we are met by what seems to
> be an immense difficulty. We have seen that perme-
> ability depends on the effect of Qh, and the ψ
> neurones are already impermeable. With still
> smaller Qh, the ω neurones would have to be still
> more impermeable. But that is a characteristic
> that we cannot grant to the vehicles of conscious-
> ness. The mutability of their content, the transi-
> toriness of consciousness, the easy linking of
> qualities simultaneously perceived--all of this
> tallies only with complete permeability of the ω
> neurones, together with total *restitutio in integrum*
> [restoration of their former state].[39]

Thus, in order to maintain his model and remain true to his basic assumptions, Freud must explain how the ω neurones can remain highly cathected, impermeable to Qh, and yet highly permeable to the small quantities of Qh associated with con-sciousness. He attempts to save himself by introducing another characteristic of the transmission of Qh, namely, that it has a temporal dimension as well as a quantitative one. He terms this temporal dimension of Qh its "period." Since qualities cannot reside in the world, it must be that their specific energy, the periodic transmission in the ω neurones, derives from the sense-organs which act as sieves both to screen out too large Q's and to transfer specific periods to the apparatus. While this concept of "period" appears to be a reasonable model for the transmission of physical energies,[40] the way Freud uses it has a rather ad hoc quality about it.

More importantly, in proposing that the energy processes of conscious experiencing, which would seem to be the primary

data scientific psychology should explain, are uniquely different than nonconscious psychological processes, Freud seems to
fail his major goal, namely of explaining psychological phenomena in purely physiological terms.[41] Indeed, in the third
section of the "Project," in a discussion of the way in which
the mechanism of attention to indications of quality functions,
Freud confesses that he cannot adequately represent how this
process operates in primary defense using the reflex-mechanism
model.[42]

Active and Passive Cathexes--the Origins of Ego Energy

"Cathexis" is Strachey's coined word to translate Freud's
very common word *Besetzung* which derives from *sitzen*, to sit,
"a static enough term!" as Holt notes.[43]

Even in the "Project," Freud used the term in two very
different ways: (1) *Cathexis* = filled with Q (or energy).[44]
For example:

> If we combine this account of the neurones with the
> conception of the Qh theory, we arrive at the idea of
> a *cathected* neurone filled with a certain Qh while
> at other times it may be empty.[45]

> If we think of a neurone filled with Qh--that is,
> cathected--we can only assume that this Q [*sic*] is
> uniform over all the regions of the neurone, and
> therefore over all its contact barriers as well.[46]

> It would seem as though the characteristic of qual-
> ity (that is, conscious sensation) comes about only
> where quantities are so far as possible excluded.
> It cannot be got rid of entirely, since we must
> think of the ω neurones too as cathected with Qh and
> striving towards discharge.[47]

> Since ω is assumed to be filled from ψ, the hypo-
> thesis would follow that when the level in ψ rises
> the cathexis in ω increases, and when, on the other
> hand, that level falls the cathexis diminishes.[48]

Now, up to this point, the way in which Freud uses the
term is fairly clear and it corresponds to the concept "inter-
cellular tetanus" which Exner had used to describe the state
of two cells that were simultaneously occupied by excitation.[49]
But, as Holt remarks, "From the beginning, Freud was concerned

with the restraint of the passions,"[50] and "A constant theme in
his theorizing is to provide some way to account for this inhibition of impulse."[51]

In order to do this, Freud rather subtly enlarged the
scope of the neurone model and, at the same time, expanded the
use of the concept cathexis by emphasizing the "force" which
cathected neurones could exert upon the stream of impulses.
Thus the term "cathexis" comes to denote an active aspect of
the apparatus as well as the passive. And this, I suggest,
amounts to a second and much more active meaning to the term.

(2) *"Once again, cathexis is here shown to be equivalent,
as regards the passage of Qh, to facilitation."*[52] He had already noted that, "...a Qh passes more easily from a neurone to
a cathected neurone than to an uncathected one."[53] Now each of
these considerations follows, logically, from his notion of the
increase in facilitation (= transmission of Qh), which occurs
in the vicinity of cathected neurones.

However, it seems to me that his next statement on the
nature of the flowing of Qh adds to the static, facilitative,
aspects of the cathected neurones, a quite new notion that the
cathected neurones themselves exert a kind of *attraction* upon
the current of Qh even from a distance.

> Here, therefore, we become acquainted with a second
> important factor in directing the course taken by
> the passage of Qh. A Qh in neurone α will go not
> only in the direction of the barrier which is best
> facilitated, but also [it will go] in the direction
> of the barrier which is cathected from the further
> side. The two factors may support each other or
> may in some cases operate against each other.[54]

Now this is a major addition to the concept of cathexis, for
Freud here makes it clear that this second attribute of the
cathected neurones, the ability to attract Qh across the space
of the cell or the hypothesized "contact" barriers, can operate
counter to, that is, against the original tendency for Qh to
seek that barrier which is most facilitated.

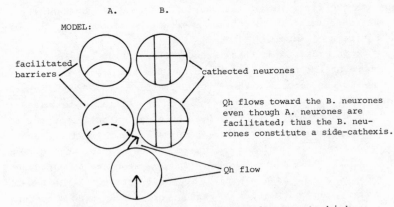

MODEL:

A.   B.

facilitated
barriers

cathected neurones

Qh flows toward the B. neurones
even though A. neurones are
facilitated; thus the B. neurones constitute a side-cathexis.

Qh flow

    I suggest that this is the fundamental concept which
underlies both the passage on "reality testing and repetition"
and the very central, though murky, concept "the attraction of
the repressed." Also, it is basic to Freud's developed notion
of *ego inhibition*, and, as I suggest, forms the first attempt,
in the physiological model (cf., 1895 text on hysteria), to
account for "counter-cathexis," "hyper-cathexis," and, much
later, "ego energies" as forces which may be alligned against
the drives (Qh currents).

    The concept of "side-cathexis" and its ability to attract
free energy (Qh) to the set of cathected (bound) neurones has a
family resemblance to the concept of "attraction of the
repressed" which Freud first described in *The Interpretation of
Dreams*.[55]

> We have put forward the view that in all probability
> this regression [in the dream work], wherever it may
> occur, is an effect of a resistance opposing the
> progress of a thought into consciousness along the
> normal path, and of a simultaneous attraction exer-
> cised upon the thought by the presence of memories
> possessing great sensory force.[56]

He adds a footnote that clarifies his meaning: "...a thought
becomes repressed as a result of the combined influence of *two*
factors. It is pushed from the one side (by the censorship of
the *Cs*.) and pulled from the other (by the *Ucs*.), in the same
kind of way in which people are conveyed to the top of the
Great Pyramid."[57]

In a later section of the same work, he proposes that
highly cathected ideas in general, regardless of their position
within the topographical systems, may exert an attraction upon
neutral associated ideas and, given sufficient scope, lose
their dangerous intensity.

> A train of thought that has been set going like this
> [= received hypercathexis] may either cease spontan-
> eously or persist. We picture the first of these
> outcomes as implying that the energy attaching to
> the train of thought is diffused along all the asso-
> ciative paths that radiate from it....[58]

These associative paths act as side-cathexes in the way he
proposed in "The Project." However, he goes on to say that
there may be purposive ideas, "lurking in our preconscious,
however...., which are derived from sources in our unconscious
and from wishes which are always on the alert."[59] Now these
wishes may exert an attractive force upon the preconscious
train of thought, "transfer" their energy onto it and thereby
prevent it from dissipating or becoming diffused.

> Thence forward the neglected or suppressed train of
> thought is in a position to persist, though the rein-
> forcement it has received gives it no right of entry
> into consciousness. We may express this by saying
> that what has hitherto been a preconscious train of
> thought has now been "drawn into the unconscious."[60]

Ego "Energy"

It is this as yet unnamed ability of cathected (tonically
"filled") neurones to attract the stream of free flowing Qh
which Freud quickly attributes to the "ego" and which, as Holt
notes,[61] he uses to explain the ego's ability to "inhibit"
discharge.

> A Qh which breaks into a neurone from anywhere will
> proceed in the direction of the contact barrier with
> the largest facilitation and will set up a current
> in that direction....Thus the course taken is depen-
> dent on Qh and the relation of the facilitations.
> We have, however, come to know the third powerful
> factor. If an adjoining neurone is simultaneously
> cathected, this acts like a temporary facilitation
> of the contact barrier lying between the two, and
> modifies the course (of the current), which would
> otherwise have been directed towards the one
> facilitated contact-barrier. A side-cathexis thus
> acts as *an inhibition of the course of Qh.*[62]

From here, Freud can follow out theimplications of this model
and use it to explain how the ego, which is a group of such
cathected neurones, can exert influence upon the primary tendency of Qh to seek immediate discharge; "Therefore, if an ego
exists, it must *inhibit* psychical primary processes."[63]

Primary Defense (Ego Attention and Attention Cathexis)

In a very shorthand way (which is expanded upon in the
third section of the "Project") Freud also goes on to explain
the notions of primary defense, and he introduces a subtle
mechanistic explanation of the ego's ability to counter painful
stimuli (including memories). If, he explains, a particular
current of Qh flowing in is on its way to a key neurone which
would release "primary unpleasure," that is, excessive Q's into
the system, the ego avoids that unpleasure by developing a
side-cathexis which can attract the flow of Qh to nonhostile
neurones.

> It is easy now to imagine how, with the help of a
> mechanism which draws the ego's *attention* to the
> imminent fresh cathexis of the hostile mnemic image,
> the ego can succeed in inhibiting the passage of
> (quantity) from a mnemic image to a release of un-
> pleasure by a copious side-cathexis which can be
> strengthened according to need.[64]

Now, I should like to emphasize that in this passage Freud
introduces a motivational, active, character to the ego which
is not evident in the original mechanistic model. He violates
his original assumptions (the six principles listed above) and
his stated aims, to erect a physiological psychology by proposing this essentially psychological notion of "attention"
and "primary defense."

As I suggested above, Freud's reasoning is very compact
and it is often necessary to tease out his meanings and the
implications of his additions to the basic model. As Rapaport
noted, "The conception of 'bound cathexes,' though it is central to the cathectic theory of psychoanalysis, refers to one
of the least understood psychoanalytic observations."[65]

Indeed, not only does this new conception of these particular neurones' ability to "bind the flow of Qh" introduce,

rather covertly, a new kind of "energy" in the system ("binding
energy"), it also contradicts the initial model of the mechanism as a simple tension-reducing apparatus. Not only is the
ego a mass of constantly cathected neurones which do not seek
discharge (though the "key neurones" are also "cathected" they
do seek discharge), the ego can expand its territory. This
fact requires one to conclude that it can counter the "original
trend" of the system to keep Qh levels to a minimum.

> If the level of cathexis in the ego-nucleus rises,
> the extent of the ego will be able to expand its
> range; if it (the level) sinks, the ego will narrow
> concentrically.[66]

Freud elegantly accounts for the source of the ego's "side-
cathexis" by supposing that "the original Qh release of unpleasure is taken up by the ego itself"[67] and this then provides
the source of energy needed to effect the side-cathexis. And
"in that case, the stronger the unpleasure, the stronger will
be the primary defense."[68]

We see here the original conception of "primary defense"
and the importance of "binding excessive stimuli" which Freud
used in his explanation of war neurosis (*Beyond the Pleasure
Principle*, Chapter III). The ego cannot bind excessive stimuli
without attaining a certain level in its own cathexis (it must
be a certain "size" in order to work).

Repetition, Hallucination, and Reality Testing

We can best explicate these three concepts by detailing
Freud's discussion of the experience of satisfaction.

Freud followed the lead of his teachers, Brücke and Exner,
as well as a detailed description by Meynert of "the experience
of satisfaction,"[69] and proposed that, originally, physiological needs and their psychological concomitants, desires, were
functions of the organism's basic tendency to reflexively perceive and then discharge stimuli arising both from within
(e.g., the appetites or drives) and from without. According to
this notion, increasing pressure of stimuli towards discharge
issues in random body movements, e.g., the infant screams and
kicks. When an external source (mother) succeeds in reducing

the painful state by effecting necessary environmental changes,
the total event constitutes an experience of satisfaction.

> For three things occur in the ψ system: (1) a lasting
> discharge is effected and so the urgency which had
> produced unpleasure in ω is brought to an end; (2) a
> cathexis of one (or several) of the neurones which
> correspond to the perception of an object occur in
> the pallium; and (3) at other points of the pallium
> information arrives of the discharge of the released
> reflex movement which follows upon the specific ac-
> tion. A facilitation is then formed between these
> cathexes and the nuclear neurones.[70]

Now, as already demonstrated, once there has been facilitation
between two or more neurones, "a" and "b", if either of those
neurones is recathected, for example by return of hunger pains,
facilitation will flow from "a" to "b" and hence there will be
a psychological association and physiological connection between the painful state (hunger), the formerly need-satisfying
object (e.g., the breast) and the memory of subsequent satisfaction. Thus when the infant is hungry again it will necessarily entertain the memory-image of the breast and then initiate discharge against the background of that hallucinated
image. But, when its hunger pains persist, Qh level rises
again and the infant experiences psychic pain. Hence the organism must be educated to reality, and Freud cranks up his model
to produce an explanation of the way in which the group of ψ
neurones (the ego) learn to discriminate between hallucinated
images and the actual (real) need-satisfying object.

In order to do this, however, he must revert back to his
notion that there is a distinct neurone system, the ω neurones,
which is impermeable to the current of Qh.

> Both wishful cathexis and release of unpleasure,
> where the memory in question is cathected anew, can
> be biologically detrimental....Here once again, then,
> it is a question of an indication to distinguish
> between a perception and a memory (idea).

> It is probably the ω neurones which furnish this
> indication: the *indication of reality*. In every case
> of external perception a qualitative excitation oc-
> curs in ω, which in the first instance, however, has
> no significance for ψ....The information of the dis-
> charge from ω is thus the indication of quality or
> reality for ψ.[71]

As already explained, the ego derives both the energy and impetus to scrutinize the discharge from ω neurones from the excessive flow of Qh brought about by nonsatisfaction. Thus, attention cathexis serves the ego's task of testing the reality-value of various images. This ability, in conjunction with the fact that the ego can deploy side-cathexis to siphon off an excessive flow of Qh, forms the basis of the secondary processes.

> Wishful cathexis to the point of hallucination (and)
> complete generation of unpleasure which involves a
> complete expenditure of defense are described by us
> as *psychical primary processes*; by contrast, those
> processes which are only made possible by a good
> cathexis of the ego, and which represent a modera-
> tion of the foregoing, are described as *psychical
> secondary processes.*[72]

Repetition and Reparation

Freud uses the distinction between primary process and secondary process and the notion of "side cathexis" to explain what was then a very puzzling feature of hysteria; namely, patients exhibited unintelligible and excessive affect around seemingly neutral ideas or memories.[73] Freud explains this mystery by demonstrating that the apparently neutral idea or memory really symbolizes or stands for an actual sexual trauma that occurred prior to sexual maturity. Thus a young woman may exhibit hysteric symptoms when in the presence of clothing store clerks because she had been sexually assaulted as a child under similar circumstances[74] even though she was not traumatized by that assault at that time.

Rather, Freud claims, the memory of the original assault becomes traumatic following the upsurge in sexual feelings at puberty.

> Although it does not usually happen in psychical life
> that a memory arouses an affect which it did not give
> rise to as an experience, this is nevertheless some-
> thing quite usual in the case of a sexual idea, pre-
> cisely because the retardation of puberty is a general
> characteristic of the organization.[75]

        This explanation obviously represents one aspect of the
original theory of hysteria which Freud had to abandon shortly
afterwards when he discovered that not all hysterics had had
prepubertal (actual) traumata.[76] However, in the same discussion, he introduces the distinction between the ego's
avoidance of unpleasure and the ego's task of creating side-
cathexis in order to repair a breech in the mechanism itself.
While he does not introduce the full-fledged notion of a stimulus barrier as he did in *Beyond the Pleasure Principle*, it is
clear that he conceives of the ego as necessarily suffering
repeated unpleasure in order to (actively) effect the necessary
side-cathexes which will prevent subsequent massive and dis-
rupting repetition of the original trauma (what he calls a
"posthumous primary affective experience").

> If the trauma (experience of pain) occurs...at a time
> when there is already an ego, there is to begin with
> a release of unpleasure, but simultaneously the ego
> is at work too, creating side-cathexes. If the
> cathexis of the memory is repeated, the unpleasure
> is repeated too, but the ego-facilitations are there
> already as well; experience shows that the release
> (of unpleasure) is less the second time, until,
> after further repetition, it shrivels up to the
> intensity of a signal acceptable to the ego.[77]

NOTES

CHAPTER IV

[1]See Amacher, *Freud's Neurological Education*.

[2]S. Bernfeld, "Freud's Earliest Theories and the School of Helmholtz," *Psychoanalytic Quarterly* 13 (1944) 341-362.

[3]Ibid.; idem, "Sigmund Freud, M.D., 1882-1885," *International Journal of Psycho-Analysis* 32 (1951) 204-217.

[4]Quoted by Jones, *Life and Work*, 1.368. Also see J. Hughlings Jackson, "On Affections of Speech from Disease of the Brain," *Brain* 1 (1878) 304-330, especially 306; and Sigmund Freud, Appendix B to "The Unconscious," *SE* 14 (1957 [1915e]) 161-215, especially 207.

[5]Rapaport, *Structure of Psychoanalytic Theory*, 43-46.

[6]Ibid., 23-24.

[7]The notion of regression figures into Freud's explanation of dreams (*Interpretation of Dreams*; "A Metapsychological Supplement to the Theory of Dreams," *SE* 14 [1957 [1917d]] 219-235), neurosis ("Fragment of an Analysis of a Case of Hysteria," *SE* 7 [1953 (1905e)] 3-122); psychosis ("Neurosis and Psychosis," *SE* 19 [1961 (1924b)] 149-153; "The Loss of Reality in Neurosis and Psychosis," *SE* 19 [1961 (1924e)] 183-187); group behavior and crowd phenomena (*Group Psychology and the Analysis of the Ego*, *SE* 18 [1955 (1921c)] 69-143); religious beliefs and practices (*Totem and Taboo*; *The Future of an Illusion*; and *Moses and Monotheism*, *SE* 23 [1964 (1939a)] 3-137); aesthetic and emotional experiences (*Jokes and Their Relation to the Unconscious*, *SE* 8 [1960 (1905c)]; "Humor," *SE* 21 [1961 (1927d)] 159-166); war ("Thoughts for the Times on War and Death," *SE* 14 [1957 (1915b)] 275-300); *Why War?*, *SE* 22 [1964 (1933b)] 197-215); creativity ("Creative Writers and Day-Dreaming," *SE* 9 [1959 (1908a)] 143-153); and, perhaps most significantly, psychoanalytic cure ("The Dynamics of Transference," *SE* 12 [1958 (1912b)] 99-108; "Recommendations to Physicians Practising Psycho-Analysis," *SE* 12 [1958 (1912e)] 111-120; "On Beginning the Treatment (Further Recommendations on the Technique of Psycho-Analysis, I)," *SE* 12 [1958 (1913c)] 123-144; "Remembering, Repeating and Working-Through (Further Recommendations on the Technique of Psycho-Analysis, II)," *SE* 12 [1958 (1914g)] 147-156; "Observations on Transference-Love (Further Recommendations on the Technique of Psycho-Analysis, III)," *SE* 12 [1958 (1915a)] 159-171; and "Analysis Terminable and Interminable," *SE* 23 [1964 (1937c)] 211-253).

[8]Jones, *Life and Work*, 1.41.

[9]D. Cardwell, *From Watt to Clausius; the Rise of Thermodynamics in the Early Industrial Age* (Ithaca: Cornell University, 1971) 258-260.

[10]Freud, *Why War?*, 197.

[11]R. W. White, *Ego and Reality in Psychoanalytic Theory*, Psychological Issues, no. 11 (New York: International Universities, 1963).

[12]Holt, "Freud's Biological Assumptions."

[13]Barros' work, "Thermodynamic and Evolutionary Concepts in the Formal Structure of Freud's Metapsychology," is especially important to this issue.

[14]Freud, "A Project for a Scientific Psychology," 325-327.

[15]Idem, "Instincts and Their Vicissitudes," *SE* 14 (1957 [1915c]) 111-140, especially 119.

[16]Idem, "Mourning and Melancholia," 244.

[17]Sigmund Freud, "Negation," *SE* 19 (1961 [1925h]) 235-239.

[18]Ibid., 236-237.

[19]Sigmund Freud, *Civilization and Its Discontents*, *SE* 21 (1961 [1930a]) 59-145.

[20]Ricoeur, *Freud and Philosophy*, 327.

[21]Freud, "A Project for a Scientific Psychology," 295.

[22]Ibid., 296.

[23]The original manuscript has "Qη" which I have consistently rendered as "Qh."

[24]Freud, "A Project for a Scientific Psychology," 298.

[25]Ibid., 299.

[26]Ibid. For a brilliant expansion of this image, see Freud's little essay, "A Note Upon the 'Mystic Writing-Pad,'" *SE* 19 (1961 [1925a]) 227-232.

[27]Freud, "A Project for a Scientific Psychology," 300.

[28]Ibid.

[29]Ibid.

[30]Freud identifies the φ neurones with the grey matter of the spinal cord "which is alone in contact with the external world," and he identifies the ψ neurones with the grey matter of the brain "which has no peripheral connections" ("A Project for a Scientific Psychology," 303).

[31]Ibid., 306.

[32]Ibid., 307.

[33]Ibid., 321. Freud maintained this basic quantified
model of psychic pain even in the later texts devoted to elaboration of the structural concepts. Thus in *The Ego and the Id*
and *Inhibitions, Symptoms, and Anxiety* he makes it clear that
the ego generates anxiety (which is a kind of unpleasure) when
it anticipates massive economic disturbance due to instinctual
upsurge, object loss, or the superego's threat of castration.

[34]Amacher notes that Freud was somewhat original in his
attempt to locate this very important psychological function
within the framework of a neurology: "Brücke, Meynert, and
Exner had simply assumed that conscious processes were the con-
comitant of cortical functioning, without specifying what part
of the cortex had the unique function of serving consciousness"
(*Freud's Neurological Education*, 65).

[35]Freud, "A Project for a Scientific Psychology," 308.

[36]Ibid., 308-309.

[37]Indeed, Freud, as Strachey notes, had many difficulties
with this section of the paper and he rearranged the sequence
of systems a few months later and placed the ω system between
the φ and ψ systems (ibid., 310, n. 3.

[38]Ibid., 309.

[39]Ibid.

[40]B. Glick, "Freud, the Problem of Quality and the
'Secretory Neuron,'" *Psychoanalytic Quarterly* 35 (1966) 84-97.

[41]Freud never abandoned this notion of "period" and he put
it forth again in *Beyond the Pleasure Principle* and "The Economic Problem of Masochism," *SE* 19 (1961 [1924c]) 157-170.

[42]I do not mean to say that he abandons his reductionistic
intentions nor that he straightforwardly engages in psychological theorizing. He does the latter in *The Interpretation of
Dreams* and he prevents the former by hypothesizing biological
rules of development which the organism learns through experience: "For the ego, then, *the biological rule of attention runs:
If an indication of reality appears, then the perceptual cathexis which is simultaneously present is to be hypercathected*"
(371).

[43]Holt, "Freud's Concept of Bound vs. Free Cathexis," 482.
Strachey concocted the English word "cathexis" from the Greek
word, κατεχειν, which means "to occupy." Strachey also notes
that Freud reconciled himself to the term which he first dis-
dained, for he used it in his Encyclopedia article (Strachey,
"The Emergence of Freud's Fundamental Hypotheses," *SE* 3 [1962]
62-68, 63 n. 3 [published as "Psycho-Analysis: Freudian
School"], *SE* 20 [1959 (1926f)] 261-270).

[44]Freud, "A Project for a Scientific Psychology," 380-381.

[45]Ibid., 298.

[46]Ibid., 301.

[47]Ibid., 3.09.

[48]Ibid., 312.

[49]Amacher, *Freud's Neurological Education*, 64.

[50]Holt (ibid., 484) carefully reviewed the notions of bound and free cathexis in the "Project" and other metapsychological essays and he warns that Freud did not use the term in the full-fledged active sense of the later essays. I agree. But, as I demonstrate above, there is a great deal of activity, perhaps latently posited, in the notions which Freud does put forth about the ability of laterally cathected neurones to "attract" free-flowing Qh.

[51]Ibid.

[52]Freud, "A Project for a Scientific Psychology," 319.

[53]Ibid.

[54]Ibid.

[55]As I shall try to indicate below in the section on the papers on metapsychology, this concept persists in Freud's fundamental theory of repression. In *Three Essays on the Theory of Sexuality* he explains the nature of hysteric amnesia in much the same way he did in the "Project":
"Hysteria amnesia, which occurs at the bidding of repression, is only explicable by the fact that the subject is already in possession of a store of memory-traces which have been withdrawn from conscious disposal, and which are now, by an associative link, attracting to themselves the material which the forces of repression are engaged in repelling from consciousness." (*Three Essays*, 175)
In turn, the notion of the attraction of the repressed is intimately related to the theory of "primary repression" which Freud developed most explicitly in the papers on metapsychology, especially "Repression" and "The Unconscious."

[56]Freud, *Interpretation of Dreams*, 547.

[57]Ibid., n. 2.

[58]Ibid., 594.

[59]Ibid.

[60]Ibid.

[61] Holt, "Freud's Concept of Bound vs. Free Cathexis," 485.

[62] Freud, "A Project for a Scientific Psychology," 323.

[63] Ibid., 324.

[64] Ibid. Holt notes that Freud enlarges the meaning of the term "binding" (*binden*) which originally referred to the fact that neurones held a large amount of cathexis (tonic excitation in the old sense) to also refer to the inhibiting effect (*hemmen*) which the group of cathected neurones exert upon the free flow of Qh ("Freud's Concept of Bound vs. Free Cathexis," 486).

[65] David Rapaport, *Organization and Pathology of Thought: Selected Sources* (New York: Columbia University, 1951) 353 n. 13. Holt lists fourteen distinct ways in which Freud used the term "bound" and "free cathexis" ("Freud's Concept of Bound vs. Free Cathexis," 512-515).

[66] Freud, "A Project for a Scientific Psychology," 370.

[67] Ibid., 324.

[68] Ibid.

[69] Amacher, *Freud's Neurological Education*, 68-69.

[70] Freud, "A Project for a Scientific Psychology," 318.

[71] Ibid., 325.

[72] Ibid., 326-327.

[73] Ibid., 348-349.

[74] Ibid., 353-356.

[75] Ibid., 356.

[76] Strachey notes that this was Freud's dominant view on the aetiology of hysteria throughout this early period and he only abandoned it when he discovered the reality of infantile sexuality (ibid., n. 1).

[77] Ibid., 359.

CHAPTER V

THE SECOND PERIOD--THE INTERPRETATION OF DREAMS

In this, his most significant work, Freud abandoned both
the full-fledged reductionistic program of the "Project" and
the steely objectivity of that earlier text. By his choice of
title and by his forthright declarations, he rejected the
physicalist's program he had attempted to carry out there.
This is not to say that he abandoned the ideal of scientific
explanation of psychological states, but in his review of the
scientific literature on dreams he makes it clear that he does
not accept their nearly universal denial that dreams are meaningful thought processes.

> As we have seen, the scientific theories of dreams
> leave no room for any problems of interpreting them,
> since in their view a dream is not a mental act at
> all, but a somatic process signalizing its occurrence
> by indications registered in the mental apparatus.[1]

Freud devotes most of his text to interpreting actual
dreams, including his own, and to surveying the phenomenon in
all of its manifest complexity, without prejudgment or pre-
selection. Thus, for the most part, the text is composed of
low-level formulations and typologies (e.g., Chapter VI on the
dream work) into which Freud attempts to place the range of
dream specimens he is familiar with. However, in its celebrated
seventh chapter, he offers a rather fragmented and, compared to
the arguments in the "Project," a rather brief metapsychology
of the dream process; "It is only after we have disposed of
everything that has to do with the work of interpretation that
we can begin to realize the incompleteness of our psychology
of dreams."[2]

In this last chapter he offers very few new thoughts on
the nature of psychic pain, repetition, and hallucination, and
the pleasure-unpleasure series. Indeed, compared to the
theoretically rich "Project," the seventh chapter is especially
deficient in its discussion of the economic considerations of
the high-level theory, especially with regard to the concepts

of cathexis and energy transformations. However, we can see
that Freud made important advances in three areas related to
the metapsychology of ritual. Those three lines of advance are:

1. A new emphasis upon motivational factors in disease
   processes,
2. A more sophisticated model of self-regulation, and
3. An elaboration of the notion of "inner reality."

Motivational Factors in Disease Processes: Wishes and Wish-Fulfillment

Thanks to the publication of Freud's letters to Fliess[3]
and Rapaport's researches into the history of ego psychology,[4]
we can summarize the major shifts which occurred in Freud's
thinking around the time of the dream book by the following
chart.

Phase I (including the "Project")	Phase II (*Interpretation of Dreams*)
Theory of Neurotogenesis Physical trauma Ego passivity Mechanistic workings Unpleasure principle	*Theory of Neurotogenesis* Psychological fixation Ego activity Psychological motives Pleasure principle

Treatment
Focused on overt pathology
Abreaction of "pent up
    energies"
	Treatment
	Focused on thought processes,
	    dreams, associations, etc.,
	    and interpretation of the
	    secret meanings of symptoms

In shifting his theoretical interests and treatment tech-
niques away from the hydraulic metaphors of the "Project" and
toward the interpretation of symptoms, Freud took a major step
toward establishing psychoanalysis both as a general psychology
(for all people dream) and as a revolutionary science which
promised to uncover the secret identity which linked the normal
life of respectable persons with the abnormal behaviors of the
mentally ill. In the book's last chapter, Freud underlines
what he considers to be his most significant and incontestable
discovery.

If we restrict ourselves to the minimum of new knowl-
ledge which has been established with certainty, we
can still say this of dreams: they have proved that
*what is suppressed continues to exist in normal people
as well as abnormal, and remains capable of psychical
functioning.*[5]

He had already shown, in Chapter VI, "The Dream Work,"
how the various distortions, symbolizations, and reshaping of
materials which occurs in all dreams were essentially identical
to those processes which produce hysteric symptoms. By emphasizing the degree to which dreams are hallucinatory wish-
fulfillments that entail structural and chronological regression, Freud could show that these everyday thought processes
were similar to those which, up to that time, had been ascribed
only to the most severe kinds of mental disorder.[6] As we have
seen in our analysis of the 1907 essay on religious acts, it
was from this low-level clinical theory that Freud went on to
generate his metapsychological formulations on the relation between individual and group dynamics. Thus the truncated theory
building of *The Interpretation of Dreams* provided an essential
link between the narrow clinical discoveries of the nineties
and the much grander psychology of culture which began with
Three Essays on the Theory of Sexuality, and the 1907 essays on
religion, "Obsessive Actions and Religious Practices" and "The
Sexual Enlightenment of Children."[7]

Finally, as we shall see more fully below, in his extremely
metaphorical treatment of dream psychology, Freud consistently
describes the various agencies and powers which conflict with
one another and which produce the manifest dream in personalis-
tic and motivational terms, e.g., the censorship. Indeed, the
quintessential psychoanalytic notion of "overdetermination of
psychical products," which Freud elaborates in the dream book,
institutionalizes a multi-motivational analysis of all psychic
functioning, normal as well as abnormal.[8]

Censorship and Overdetermination

In attempting to clarify Freud's meaning we run directly
into what Ricoeur aptly calls the "two languages" of Freudian
metapsychology: the language of hermeneutics and the language
of energetics. The former mode of discourse is akin to the
therapeutic work of interpreting dream materials to the patient
as if they were puzzles, or secrets which had been distorted in
order to escape condemnation (see Chapters II, III, IV, and V
of *The Interpretation of Dreams*). The latter mode of discourse

pertains to the scientific task of explaining, within the six
assumptions mentioned above, the mechanisms which might bring
about such distortion and hence the need for interpretation.
Freud consistently alternates between these "two languages" in
Chapter VII of the dream book and therefore central concepts,
such as censorship, manifest according to Ricoeur a kind of
dual nature.[9]

Freud first used the term "censorship" in the technical
chapter of *Studies on Hysteria* in which he describes how he
came to recognize that part of his patient's mind actively and
willfully resisted his efforts at cure. He found that by
pressing their foreheads and telling them they would thereby
recall the significant traumatic scene which was the source of
their present symptoms his patients would recall formerly un-
available memories.[10]

If we can visualize Freud leaning over his patient and
insisting that she remember while he presses her forehead, we
see a fully set stage in which a dramatic, even histrionic conflict between the two persons is played out for the benefit of
those ideas and memories which willfully resist communicating
with the external world. In this case, the private relationship between doctor and patient completely corresponds to the
very private relationship between the censored and censoring
parts of the patient's mind.

Having hypothesized the existence of conflict within the
patient analogous to that which occurs between the doctor and
his patient, Freud goes on to suggest that we can further hy-
pothesize that there exists a kind of internal censorship which
controls both what a person receives or perceives from his external environment and his access to memories, and other presentations in his internal environment. Freud resists specu-
lating on the location and mechanisms responsible for such external and internal censoring. Instead he reverts to clinical
examples to clarify what he intends by the term.

> I will give one or two examples of the way in which a
> censoring of this kind operates when pathogenic
> recollections first emerge. For instance, the pa-
> tient sees the upper part of a woman's body [when
> Freud applies his hand to the patient's forehead]

with the dress not properly fastened--out of care-
lessness, it seems. It is not until much later that
he fits a head to this torso and thus reveals a
particular person and his relationship to her.[11]

The essentially descriptive-clinical way in which Freud
uses the term here, and in his essay, "The Neuro-Psychoses of
Defence,"[12] corresponds to the way in which he uses it in the
dream book in those chapters devoted to interpretation. However, as already mentioned, in Chapter VII of the dream book
he goes beyond the work of interpretation.

...we shall be obliged to set up a number of fresh
hypotheses which touch tentatively upon the structure
of the apparatus of the mind and the play of forces
operating in it.[13]

The hypotheses about the operation of the censorship, for
example, which Freud puts forward are not absolutely fresh, for
they consistently reflect the model of mental functioning he
had already worked out in the "Project," of which only he and
Fliess were aware. The underlying model which he employs to
explain "censorship" is based on his fundamental notion that
all thoughts, memory traces, indeed all psychic contents have
both an ideational (representational) aspect and an energetic
aspect. Thus, the censorships which one can observe functioning both in dreams and in production of memory gaps in neurotic
patients can carry out their missions, that of disguising or
blocking out certain thoughts from awareness, in two ways: they
can distort the representational content of the idea (e.g., by
symbolization or by editing out key concepts), or they can
allow the full content to pass but divert the energy (quota of
affect) originally associated with that idea by displacement
or other means of diversion.

Thus the twofold nature of all thought processes corresponds to the twofold operation of the various censorships and
to the modes of defense which are associated with them. Now,
although Freud avowed that he did not wish to found his dream
psychology on his work in psychopathology, shortly into Chapter
VII he admits that he cannot make sense of the former without
recourse to the latter.[14] The essence of his early work on
hysteria is, again, that all psychical products have a larger

or smaller quota of affect (psychic energy, "Qh") associated
with them. We can see many of the essential features of his
work on psychopathology and the essential theorem of the dual-
ity of mental contents in a very early paper, "Some Points for
a Comparative Study of Organic and Hysterical Motor Paralysis,"[15]
originally written in French at the suggestion of Charcot.

In this paper Freud notes, following Janet, that the extent
of paralysis used by organic lesions is a function of anatomical
connections, while "...*in its paralyses and other manifestations
hysteria behaves as though anatomy did not exist or as though
it had no knowledge of it.*"[16] On the contrary, as occurs in
hypnotically induced amnesia, hysteric symptoms seem to reflect,
in their extent and location, an everyday popular conception of
the body and body parts "...not founded on a deep knowledge of
neuroanatomy but on our tactile and above all our visual perceptions."[17] Thus, Freud concludes, the lesion in hysteria is
not organic but psychical; it is not in the brain or other
neural structures, but in the mind, in our conceptions and
representations of our bodies. How can we explain this?

Freud reaches down into the language of energetics and the
psychology of conception for his answer.

> If the conception of the arm is involved in an asso-
> ciation with a large quota of affect, it will be in-
> accessible to the free play of other associations.
> *The arm will be paralysed in proportion to the per-
> sistence of this quota of affect or to its diminuation
> by appropriate psychical means*...in every case of
> hysterical paralyses, we find that *the paralysed
> organ or the lost function is involved in a sub-
> conscious association which is provided with a large
> quota of affect and it can be shown that the arm is
> liberated as soon as this quota is wiped out.*[18]

Although Freud was to abandon his notion that the source of this
large quota of affect was always psychical-sexual traumata,[19] he
did not abandon the rudimentary model of censorship and defense
implied in this explanation of hysteric paralysis. Indeed the
fundamental principle behind this early theory of hysteria and
all his later theories of neurotic symptoms is based upon the
assumption, mentioned above, that underlies his mixed discourse:
"Every event, every psychical impression is provided with a
certain quota of affect of which the ego divests itself either

by means of a motor reaction or by associative psychical activity."[20] Accordingly, the various censorships which seem to
distort dream productions as well as dream recall,[21] can defend
against the emergence of repressed or suppressed thoughts in
either of two ways: (1) the dream-work can distort the representation (image, thought, idea) through symbolization or other
"associated" pathways, or (2) it can displace, redirect, or
disassocate the original quota of affect (or cathectic current)
originally associated with the dangerous thoughts.

Again, Freud does not pretend to offer more than low-level
metaphorical hypotheses about the actual way in which the dream
work and the censorships function. But it is clear that by the
name and description of censoring he implies that it is more
anthropomorphized than it is mechanized. This is another reason why he dropped the full-fledged reductive language of the
"Project" and replaced it with interpretative language. For
dream interpretation is possible only if the significant aspects
of dream content are products of intentional, motivational concerns, i.e., a censorship that seeks to hide and disguise the
secrets and hidden meanings which the interpreter seeks to uncover. Thus, having claimed that the censorship is most responsible for the forgetting of dreams (not simply poor or in-
distinct memory), Freud attempts to justify the method of interpretation he evolved, free association, against those who
might criticize its apparent aimlessness.

> ...it is demonstrably untrue that we are being carried
> along a purposeless stream of ideas when, in the pro-
> cess of interpreting a dream, we abandon reflection
> and allow involuntary ideas to emerge. It can be
> shown that all that we ever get rid of are purposive
> ideas that are *known* to us; as soon as we have done
> this, *unknown*--or, as we inaccurately say, "uncon-
> scious"--purposive ideas take charge and thereafter
> determine the course of the involuntary ideas.[22]

Indeed, he immediately goes on to say that the censorship,
acting like the censors of Russian newspapers, is responsible
for the apparent nonsensical structure of dream text which interpretation reveals to be purposive in the same way that hysteric symptoms and obsessive actions are purposive.

With the publication of *The Interpretation of Dreams*,
Freud radically changed his larger conception of the mechanisms
responsible for both neurosis and neurotic-like phenomena. In
the dream book he attempts to elucidate the motivational hier-
archies which ultimately produce manifest dream content. However, in Chapter VII, on the psychology of dream formation, he
confronts a variation of the mind-body (or mind-brain) problem,
namely, how far back into time or how deeply into unconscious
processes can one interpret dream content? Must there not be
some point either in the development of the ego and its functions or in the source of dream images which is pre-
psychological?

Freud was aware of this difficulty and he attempted to
answer it on a variety of levels. For example, in his discussion of why dreams are forgotten, he puts forward the rather
obscure notion of a "dream navel."

> There is often a passage in even the most thoroughly
> interpreted dream which has to be left obscure: this
> is because we become aware during the work of inter-
> pretation that at that point there is a tangle of
> dream-thoughts which cannot be unravelled and which
> moreover adds nothing to our knowledge of the content
> of the dream. This is the dream's navel, the spot
> that reaches down into the unknown. The dream-
> thoughts to which we are led by interpretation can-
> not, from the nature of things, have any definite
> endings; they are bound to branch out in every
> direction into the intricate network of our world
> of thought.[23]

The metaphor of "dream navel" is certainly provocative.
It suggests that the dream itself is a child thrown out into
the world of consciousness and representation attached, as it
were, to a mysterious source or womb of generation and psychic
experience which is beyond our understanding. However, Freud
says a great deal more about the more basic, though allied,
concept of the wish.

The Wish--On the Border Between Mind and Body

The concept of the wish is precisely fitted to the task
and fundamental problem Freud faced in his attempt to formulate
a science of dream interpretation which could uncover hidden

meanings in apparently nonmeaningful (nonrepresentational)
dream products. On the one hand, there is ample experiential
evidence that many dreams, especially those of children, are
outright wish-fulfillments,[24] and on the other, the elaborate
theory of the experience of satisfaction from the "Project"
provided a ready explanation of the way in which somatic, nonrepresentational, drives and needs got translated into psychological contents. However, the difficulty with that latter
theory is that it is entirely developmental. Hence one must
explain sophisticated nonwishful thinking (what he termed
secondary thinking) as the products of earlier, drive-induced
attempts at, in the language of the "Project," hallucination
of the original experience of satisfaction.[25]

It is Freud's adherence to this developmental/genetic
explanation that forces him, in his discussion of types of
wishes, to make the supposition that the basic and most fundamental source of all dreams is an archaic wish, emanating from
one's earliest periods. That is, in the section of Chapter VII
on wish-fulfillment, Freud notes that one can see that most
dreams have a number of wishes and desires which come from very
different sources. He names four:

1. wishes that (consciously) arose during the day but
   weren't satisfied,
2. wishes that arose, but were suppressed,
3. wishes due to somatic tensions during the night,
   e.g., thirst, and
4. wishes that arise from the unconscious during
   sleep.

He then asks which of these is the most important source of the
dream content. He answers:

> My supposition is that a conscious wish can only become
> a dream-instigator if it succeeds in awakening an un-
> conscious wish with the same tenor and in obtaining
> reinforcement from it.[26]

As suggested above, one can find the neurological model
for this supposition in the "Project" where Freud described the
ability of cathected neurones to attract free-flowing cathexis
to themselves. However, in the dream book, he relies upon a
chain of metaphors to illustrate this otherwise unsupported
supposition.

These wishes in our unconscious, ever on the alert
and, so to say, immortal, remind one of the legendary
Titans, weighed down since primeval ages by the
massive bulk of the mountains which were once hurled
upon them by the victorious gods and which are still
shaken from time to time by the convulsion of their
limbs.[27]

By insisting upon this primarily genetic explanation of
dream production, Freud is able to make use of both the clinical theory of neurosis and the "Project's" models of the development of thought. However, all such regressive explanations
must stop somewhere. In order to avoid the trap of offering
explanations which extend backwards into infinity, Freud had to
explain how the developmental series began.[28] He indirectly
answers this criticism in two ways. First, he ameliorates the
stringency of his supposition that the most fundamental wish in
all dreams is an infantile one.

I am aware that this assertion cannot be proved to
hold universally; but it can be proved to hold frequently, even in unsuspected cases, and it cannot be
contradicted as a general proposition.[29]

Second, he distinguished between mental processes which are
truly unconscious, that is, which belong to the original, un-
differentiated system termed the *Ucs.*, from those which are
suppressed into the *Ucs*. Speaking of the former he notes:

If I may use a simile, they are only capable of anni-
hilation in the same sense as the ghosts in the under-
world of the Odyssey--ghosts which awoke to new life
as soon as they tasted blood. Processes which are
dependent on the preconscious system are destructible
in quite another sense. The psychotherapy of the
neuroses is based on this distinction.[30]

This simile is persuasive and rhetorically mirrors the archaic
qualities Freud wishes to impart to the earliest wishes of
childhood. It reinforces the metaphor of the Titans he had
just used, for the Titans were archaic powers who figure in the
origins of Greek civilization. It is not, however, very en-
lightening. The ghosts whom Odysseus attracts with the freshly-
killed sheep (Odyssey, Book 11), were once quite lively people
who now exist only as remnants, as shades. The most archaic
wishes of the *Ucs.* were, by definition, never fully realized in

consciousness; they have never seen the light of day. A few
pages later he proposes a bit more dogmatically another simile:
the *Ucs.* functions like a capitalist who lends hard cash to the
Pcs. which in turn acts as an entrepreneur and carries out the
former's original goals.

> ...the *capitalist* who can afford the outlay, and the
> capitalist who provides the psychical outlay for the
> dream is invariably and indisputably, whatever may be
> the thoughts of the previous day, *a wish from the
> unconscious.*[31]

Again, while this is a rather striking image, it hardly
clarifies or justifies Freud's central contention that the ultimate source of dream content is in every case a wish from the
unconscious, or as he says in other parts, that dreaming is a
piece of infantile life,[32] or again, that wishes derived from
the *Ucs.* are immortal and indestructible.[33] Indeed, it would
seem that such wishes are quite destructible, in the sense that
they can be fulfilled both in dream life and in some forms of
psychotic ideation. However, fulfilling such wishes, Freud is
clear to say, does not destroy them. Thus he remarks about one
of his own dreams.[34]

> I must have been prepared at all times in my *Ucs.* to
> identify myself with Professor R., since by means of
> that identification one of the immortal wishes of
> childhood--the megalamanic wish--was fulfilled.[35]

This is surely a major weakness in the theory of dreams,
and, in conjunction with the other striking inadequacies listed
above, one must note that Freud does not demonstrate why the
ultimate instigator of all dreams must be wishes from the *Ucs.*
and why these wishes must be immortal and indestructible. However, it is clear that these hypotheses conform to Freud's more
inclusive theory of thinking, as it was first worked out in the
"Project," and as it is put forth in parts E and F of the
seventh chapter.[36] Thus in the most substantial section of the
seventh chapter, part E, "The Primary and Secondary Processes--
Repression," Freud asserts again that dreams represent the re-
surgence of archaic, infantile life.

> The fact that dreams are hypermnesic and have access
> to material from childhood has become one of the
> corner-stones of our teaching. Our theory of dreams
> regards wishes originating in infancy as the indis-
> pensable motive force for the formation of dreams.[37]

After summarizing his findings regarding the phenomenological
similarities between dream content and hysteric symptoms, the
low-level clinical theory of censorship and dream-distortion,
Freud reintroduces the very high-level model of the mind as a
reflex apparatus. With little discussion and no references or
data base, Freud asserts the "Project's" major thesis that the
mechanism is regulated by pleasure-unpleasure, under the law of
constancy, and that the thing runs on wishes which are functions
of an original experience of satisfaction and act as "currents"
that aim at recreating those original conditions.

Thus even in the unsubstantiated model of the wish, we see
Freud's overriding theoretical commitment is to a regressive
explanation. Just as all dreams are finally expressions of an
archaic wish, so too all wishes are finally expressions of an
archaic real experience of satisfaction. It may not be far-
fetched to say that Freud's analysis of thinking, including
secondary thinking, follows the same reductive, regressive
model that we already saw in his analysis of repetition in
Beyond the Pleasure Principle. In the former we are told that

> all thinking is no more than a circuitous path from
> the memory of a satisfaction (a memory which has been
> adopted as a purposive idea) to an identical cathexis
> of the same memory which it hoped to attain once more
> through the intermediate stage of motor experiences.[38]

In the latter we were told that

> what appears in a minority of human individuals as an
> untiring impulsion towards further perfection can
> easily be understood as a result of the instinctual
> repression upon which is based all that is most
> precious in human civilization. The repressed in-
> stinct never ceases to strive for complete satisfac-
> tion, which would consist in the repetition of a
> primary experience of satisfaction.[39]

It was his original commitment to mechanistic, reflex-
based, models of psychic functioning, and the subsequent dialectic explanation of rational thought and rational action as

roundabout expressions of more primary processes and archaic
forms, which required Freud to first suppose and then assert
that the wishes, thoughts, and processes of the *Ucs.* are primary to all others and therefore irreplaceable.

> ...the primary processes are present in the mental
> apparatus from the first, while it is only during the
> course of life that the secondary processes unfold,
> and come to inhibit and overlay the primary ones; it
> may even be that their complete domination is not
> attained until the prime of life. In consequence
> of the belated appearance of the secondary processes,
> the core of our being, consisting of unconscious wish-
> ful impulses, remains inaccessible to the understand-
> ing and inhibition of the preconscious; the part
> played by the latter is restricted once and for all
> to directing along the most expedient paths the
> wishful impulses that arise from the unconscious.[40]

In addition to the doubtful manner of his argument, Freud's
account of the primary and secondary processes seems mechani-
cally dualistic; he often seems to reify the *Ucs.* and *Pcs.* and
to drive too hard a line between primary and secondary processes.
However, Freud's argument is much more fluid and much less
dualistic than this first reading of the chapter would admit.

Layers of Self-Regulation

In a few brief paragraphs on the nature of the interaction
between primary and secondary processes, Freud suggests that
(1) the difference between the two processes is not a function
of rigid, monolithic systems, *Pcs.* and *Ucs.* Rather, it is a
function of the degree of discharge inhibition, and (2) that
the "sense organ" of consciousness serves to moderate and
regulate primary process peremptoriness by binding immediate
discharge with its hypercathexis. It is in this context that
he makes the enigmatic distinction between thinking which aims
at establishing a perceptual identity and that which aims at
establishing a thought identity.

Thus according to Freud, when the mind is under the sway
of primary processes they endeavor to establish a "perceptual
identity," with the original experience of satisfaction,
whereas secondary process thinking aims at establishing a
"thought identity."[41]   Rapaport[42] illuminates this rather

obscure distinction by noting that, whereas "perceptual identity" in thought amounts to simply hallucinating the appearance
of the desired end state, establishing a thought identity means
that one recalls or visualizes the various steps one had to
take before one got to that end state, that is, discharge.
Thus Freud notes, "Thinking must concern itself with the con-
necting paths between ideas...."[43] A few pages later he notes
that "...from the moment at which the repressed thoughts are
strongly cathected by the unconscious wishful impulse and, on
the other hand abandoned by the preconscious cathexis, they become subject to the primary process and their one aim is motor
discharge or...*hallucinatory revival of the desired perceptual
identity.*"[44]

In order to avoid this maladaptive outcome, Freud implies
that the organism must struggle to overcome reflex action based
on the pleasure principle (which would entail both automatic
reaction against painful memory images and automatic affirma-
tion of [cathexis of] pleasure-associated memory images) such
that prior experiencing only serves as a signal of possible
outcomes of the intended action. In this way the organism can
achieve a "greater delicacy of functioning."[45] Gill analyzes
this part of the seventh chapter and he conveniently outlines
the "...series of progressively advanced regulations of psychic
functioning"[46] which Freud elaborated.

> The most primitive is an automatic regulation by the
> unpleasure principle: An advance upon this regulation
> is brought about by the regulation resulting from the
> excitation of the sense organs, and the psychical
> sense organs are *Pcpt.* [perceptual system] and *Cs.*
> [system of consciousness]. These sense organs achieve
> their purpose by directing the distribution of atten-
> tion cathexis and, more generally, of the mobile
> cathexis of the *Pcs.* The sense organ *Pcpt.* is ex-
> citable only by perceptual quality. But the sense
> organ *Cs.* is higher in the hierarchy than the sense
> organ *Pcpt.*, and it is stimulated not only by per-
> ceptual quality but also by the qualities of pleasure
> and pain.[47]

Again, we see that Freud's major conceptions of such regulation
are functions of his more primary commitment to a general developmental point of view which holds that primary modes of

thought are superseded and "controlled" both ontogenetically
and phylogenetically by the gradual development of higher
neural functions, such as consciousness, that have the ability
to direct smaller amounts of more or less neutralized energy
(cathexis) which can produce or inhibit a process of summation
and discharge. Because such high-level regulation is dependent
upon both a long history of successive and successful regulation of the drives and the lack of excessive drive demands,
"...it is only during the course of life that the secondary
processes unfold, and come to inhibit the primary ones; it may
even be that their complete domination is not attained until
the prime of life."[48]

The real mystery of the development of secondary process
thinking, however, is not simply that we can see in the formation of symptoms and the automatic features of secondary revision in dreams[49] that peremptory impulses are controlled or
inhibited to some degree. Rather, the mystery is that (1)
formerly pleasure-producing wishes of infancy no longer generate an affect of pleasure but of unpleasure,[50] and (2) secondary thought processes, that is, adaptive needs, may require
one to cathect (recall) originally pain-producing memories.[51]
As we shall see below, Freud attempted to maintain his original
theoretical orientation, the six major assumptions of his system, and account for these central features of defense and
adaptation.

The Notion of Inner Reality

In the last section of Chapter VII, Freud clearly distinguishes between the low-level, phenomenologically-based observation that much of mental life is not available to consciousness, and the high-level, theory-laden, suppositions and metaphors of the topographical considerations he had advanced. The
former is what we should like to explain, the latter is one of
many possible points of view. Indeed, Freud notes that the
economic considerations of cathectic currents are more basic
than the topographic speculations.

It will be seen on closer consideration that what the
psychological discussion of the preceding sections
invites us to assume, is not the existence of two
systems near the motor end of the apparatus but the
existence of two kinds of *processes of excitation* or
modes of its discharge. It is all one to us, for we
must always be prepared to drop our conceptual scaf-
folding if we feel that we are in a position to replace it by something that approximates more closely
to the unknown reality.[52]

That unknown reality which he aimed to explore is the unconscious which, in all of us, is larger than and contains our
fleeting consciousness.

The unconscious is the true psychical reality; *in its
innermost nature it is as much unknown to us as the
reality of the external world, and it is as incom-
pletely presented by the data of consciousness as is
the external world by communications of our sense
organs.*[53]

The study of dreams is important not just because dreams offer
clues to the origins and nature of psychopathological phenomena,
but because through their study we gain insight into the ways
in which our daily life and conscious self-knowledge depend
upon the immense forces of nature and of our own unconscious.

It is...instructive to get to know the much trampled
soil from which our virtues proudly spring. Very
rarely does the complexity of human character, driven
hither and thither by dynamic forces, submit to a
choice between simple alternatives, as our antiquated
morality would have us believe.[54]

In terms of the topographic theory, the sense organ of
consciousness resides between the system *Ucs.* and system *Pcpt.*,
which in turn contacts the real world.[55] Thus, according to
Freud, what we regard as our true selves, that is, that part of
our mental and physical life of which we are conscious, is only
a small, often weak, arbitrator between the immense forces of
the outside world, and the immensely mysterious and often
threatening forces of the inside world, the unconscious.

The significance of this vision for Freud's thought cannot
be stressed too often. The whole force of the seventh chapter
and the dream book as a whole is towards acknowledging that, in
contrast to the early papers on hysteria and the arguments of

the "Project," reality and reality demands made upon the
psychic mechanism are twofold. The conscious self must confront both the outer world of others, and of space and time,
and the inner world where space and time are suspended.

NOTES

CHAPTER V

[1]Freud, *Interpretation of Dreams*, 96.

[2]Ibid., 510-511.

[3]Freud, *Origins of Psycho-Analysis, Letters to Wilhelm Fliess*.

[4]Rapaport, *Structure of Psychoanalytic Theory*.

[5]Freud, *Interpretation of Dreams*, 608.

[6]Ibid., 567-568.

[7]Sigmund Freud, "The Sexual Enlightenment of Children," *SE* 9 (1959 [1907c]) 131-139.

[8]Freud used the term "overdetermination" (*Überdeterminiert*) in his and Breuer's *Studies on Hysteria* (212). In that text it refers to the fact that one sees a variety of energy sources contribute to the affect exhibited in hysterical attacks. Thus he writes of one of his early cases, "...the energy for the conversion had been supplied, on the one hand by freshly experienced affect and, on the other, by recollected affect" (*Studies on Hysteria*, 173). He uses the term in the later topographic and structural theories in a similar way to denote that symptoms and indeed all behavior must be seen to satisfy and represent the demands, wishes, and requirements of those structures which constitute the mental apparatus, e.g., "A [hysterical] symptom is not merely the expression of a realized unconscious wish; a wish from the preconscious which is fulfilled by the same symptom must also be present" (*Interpretation of Dreams*, 569). In a very influential essay ("The Principle of Multiple Function"), Robert Waelder modified the early "id-psychological" definitions of "overdetermination" in favor of an ego-psychological one which recognized the ego's status as the central steering mechanism which guides the organism in all its functioning, hence, "...no attempted solution of a problem is possible which is not of such a type that it does not at the same time, in some way or other, represent an attempted solution of other problems" (49).

[9]Ricoeur, *Freud and Philosophy*, 92-93.

[10]Freud, *Studies on Hysteria*, 268.

[11]Ibid., 282.

[12]Sigmund Freud, "Further Remarks on the Neuro-Psychoses of Defence," *SE* 3 (1962 [1896b]) 159-185.

[13]Idem, *Interpretation of Dreams*, 511.

119

[14]Ibid., 544-546.

[15]Sigmund Freud, "Some Points for a Comparative Study of Organic and Hysterical Motor Paralysis," *SE* 1 (1966 [1893c]) 157-172.

[16]Ibid., 169.

[17]Ibid., 170.

[18]Ibid., 171.

[19]For example, in draft K of "The Neuroses of Defence," he writes: "Hysteria necessarily presupposes a primary unpleasurable experience--that is, one of a passive kind. The natural sexual passivity of women accounts for their being more inclined to hysteria" (quoted in *Origins of Psycho-Analysis*, 154).

[20]Freud, "Comparative Study of Organic and Hysterical Motor Paralysis," 171-172.

[21]Idem, *Interpretation of Dreams*, 517.

[22]Ibid., 528.

[23]Ibid., 525.

[24]Ibid., 127-131.

[25]"An essential component of this experience of satisfaction is a particular perception (that of nourishment, in our example) the mnemic image of which remains associated thenceforward with the memory trace of the excitation produced by the need. As a result of the link that has thus been established, next time this need arises a psychical impulse will at once emerge which will seek to recathect the mnemic image of the perception and to reevoke the perception itself; that is to say, to re-establish the situation of the original satisfaction. An impulse of this kind is what we call a wish..." (ibid., 565-566).

[26]Ibid., 553.

[27]Ibid.

[28]David Rapaport ("Seminars on Elementary Metapsychology Held at the Western New England Institute for Psychoanalysis" [3 vols.; ed. Stuart C. Miller; typewritten, 1957] 301) notes the concept "primal repression" very much serves to avoid the problem of infinite regress.

[29]Freud, *Interpretation of Dreams*, 554.

[30]Ibid., 553, n. 1. Thus Freud states further on in the chapter, "...*psychotherapy can pursue no other course than to bring the Ucs. under the domination of the Pcs.*" (578).

[31]Ibid., 561.

[32]Ibid., 567.

[33]Ibid., 556.

[34]Ibid., 269.

[35]Ibid., 556.

[36]Ricoeur makes this essential point in his analysis of the seventh chapter (*Freud and Philosophy*, 105-113 and 390-400).

[37]Freud, *Interpretation of Dreams*, 589.

[38]Ibid., 602.

[39]Freud, *Beyond the Pleasure Principle*, 42.

[40]Idem, *Interpretation of Dreams*, 603.

[41]Ibid., 602.

[42]David Rapaport, "Seminars on Psychoanalytic Ego Psychology Held at the Western New England Institute for Psychoanalysis" (ed. Stuart C. Miller; typewritten, 1955) 46.

[43]Freud, *Interpretation of Dreams*, 602.

[44]Ibid., 605, my italics.

[45]Ibid., 602, 609.

[46]Gill, *Topography and Systems*, 17.

[47]Ibid., 17-18. Gill is summarizing the very condensed few pages of the last section of Chapter VII, "The Unconscious and Consciousness--Reality," especially 615-617.

[48]Freud, *Interpretation of Dreams*, 603.

[49]The secondary process functioning of the system *Pcs.* exhibits what was later called the ego's synthetic function. "The following consideration makes it highly probably that the psychical function which carries out what we have described as the secondary revision of the content of dreams is to be identified with the activity of our waking thought. Our waking (preconscious) thinking behaves towards any perceptual material with which it meets in just the same way in which the function we are considering behaves towards the content of dreams. It is the nature of our waking thought to establish order in material of that kind, to set up relations in it and to make it conform to our expectations of an intelligible whole" (ibid., 499).

[50]Ibid.

[51]Ibid., 602.

[52]Ibid., 610.

[53]Ibid., 613.

[54]Ibid., 621.

[55]"The psychical apparatus, which is turned towards the external world with its sense-organ of the *Pcpt.* systems, is itself the external world in relation to the sense-organ of the *Cs.*, whose teleological justification resides in this circumstance. Here we once more meet the principle of the hierarchy of agencies, which seems to govern the structure of the apparatus" (Freud, *Interpretation of Dreams*, 615-616). Rapaport attempted to exploit this hierarchical theorem of the mental structure in a posthumous paper in which he uses the notion of consciousness as a sense-organ ("The Theory of Attention Cathexis: An Economic and Structural Attempt at the Explanation of Cognitive Processes," pp. 778-794 in *The Collected Papers of David Rapaport* (ed. Merton Gill; New York: Basic Books, 1967).

CHAPTER VI

THE THIRD PERIOD--PAPERS ON METAPSYCHOLOGY

In the spring of 1915, Freud returns to the task of con-
solidating and systematizing the discoveries of his and other's
psychoanalytic investigations that had forged ahead of the
dream psychology of the seventh chapter of *The Interpretation
of Dreams*.

According to Jones,[1] Freud wrote a total of twelve, inter-
connected papers within a period of seven months which he hoped
would ground the new discoveries in a systematic and stable
theory base. These papers, which were to be published under
the rubric of "Preliminaries to a Metapsychology,"[2] were to
deal with major psychoanalytic themes, such as sublimation and
projection, that had not received detailed attention up to that
time. It appears Freud did write all twelve, but to our great
loss, he destroyed seven of them and thus left us less than
half the original text which, in its dissected state, contains
a number of obscure and often confounding gaps.[3] Nevertheless,
the remaining metapsychological papers[4] are extremely rich
contributions.

Taken together, the five papers systematically correlate
the dynamic, topographic, and especially economic points of
view on mental functioning and so mark a conceptual advance
over the more scattered theorems of the seventh chapter. While
it would be possible and instructive to examine the five psychoanalytic concepts related to ritual in light of that theoretical advance, there are two particular themes elaborated in
the papers which pertain most directly to our concerns. Those
two themes are: (1) Freud radically recasts the notions of
inner and outer reality, and (2) he analyzes the central problem of quality using quantitative factors and, in so doing,
elevates the function and status of repetitive behaviors. At
the end of this section, I shall suggest that these shifts both
underlie the construction of the structural essays of the last
period and provide groundwork for a more adequate analysis of
ritual actions.

The Inner World

In the first two lines of the first essay in the series,
Freud accurately implies the nature of the conceptual framework
he will propose: "We have often heard it said that sciences
should be built upon clear and sharply defined basic concepts.
In actual fact no science, not even the most exact, begins with
such definitions."[5]

Thus when, in the next breath, he goes on to propose a
definition of the psychological term "instinct" (*Trieb*), he
notes that, owing to the obscurity of the mental mechanism, we
cannot simply take over the physiological notion of stimulus as
he had proposed in the "Project." Rather he proposes that we
"imagine ourselves in the situation of an almost entirely help-
less living organism, as yet unoriented in the world...." It
is no accident that he requires us to assume this extraordinary
point of view, for it is precisely from there, within the hypothesized mental mechanism, that he begins his theorizing.[6] It
is this initial orientation, which Ricoeur brilliantly terms an
"anti-phenomenology,"[7] that allows Freud to, as it were, work
from inside the mental mechanism and explain how the mind confronts both the reality of the world and the physical body
which encapsulates it and the inner reality of the unconscious
needs and thoughts which underlie conscious mental life.

The unavoidable effect, however, of taking this point of
view is that, while it grants a kind of objectivity to the mind
or mental mechanism, it also relegates the inner and outer
worlds to the status of noumena, of realms which must now para-
doxically be explained vis-à-vis our notions about the mind and
its functioning. These are precisely the difficulties with
which we see Freud struggle: (1) what is the relationship between the mental mechanism and mental processes and the body?
and (2) what is the relationship between the mind and the world
external to the body?

Body and Mind: The Source and Representation of Instincts

In his introduction to "Instincts and Their Vicissitudes,"
Strachey notes that Freud's definition of the term "instinct"

(*Trieb*) varies from text to text. In the *Three Essays* and his discussion of the Schreber case,[8] Freud says that instincts are psychical representatives of organic forces.[9] In the first part of the 1915 essay, he maintains this definition where he writes that an instinct is "a concept on the frontier between the mental and the somatic, ...the psychical representative [*psychischer Repräsentant*] of the stimuli originating from within the organism and reaching the mind...."[10] However, he appears to confound and contradict this rather straightforward definition in the later papers, "The Unconscious," when he insists that "an instinct can never become an object of consciousness--only the idea that represents an instinct can [*nur die Vorstellung, die ihn repräsentiert*]."[11] Ricoeur focuses upon this problem and succinctly states the difficulty it presents.

> ...instincts are like the Kantian thing--the transcendental = X; they too are never attained except in that which stands for and represents them. In this way we will be led from the problematic of instincts to the problematic of the representatives of instincts.[12]

The key which unlocks this apparent contradiction between the first and third essays is, as Ricoeur suggests, contained in the middle paper, "Repression." In it Freud labors to explain how psychological experience and *psychological* verbal treatment, that is, psychoanalysis, can so drastically affect the disposition and expression of essentially *biological* processes, the instincts. Where, in the first essay on the vicissitudes of instincts, Freud spoke from a physiological-biological point of view, in "Repression" it is clear that he means to more fully describe this particular instinctual vicissitude from the point of view of clinical observation of psychological states.

> Let us...confine ourselves to clinical experience, as we meet with it in psycho-analytic practice. We then learn that the satisfaction of an instinct which is under repression would be quite possible, and further, that in every instance such a satisfaction would be pleasurable in itself; but it would be irreconcilable with other claims and intentions. It would, therefore, cause pleasure in one place and unpleasure in another.[13]

When he introduced the essentially observational, clini-
cally-based notion of repression into his metapsychological
considerations, Freud enormously complicated his theoretical
task. In Ricoeur's terms, he had to mate the language of
force, which as we have seen he derived from the physicalist-
physiological model, with the language of desire, secrecy, and
memory. Thus, in the passage quoted above, he does not maintain the physiological language of the first essay on instincts,
rather he directly implies that the mental mechanism also runs
on claims and intentions and, perhaps even more mysterious
still, there are competing and contradictory elements within it.

As I indicated above in my discussion of the concept of
the attraction of the repressed as it is first formulated in
the "Project," it is the unique ability of cathected neurones,
in the language of physiology, or of intense ideas, in language
of the dream text, to attract formerly neutral ideas to them
which underlies Freud's explanation of repression. Granted
this theoretical model, Freud then faces the task of explaining
both why repression occurs and how it, an essentially *psychological* process, can control fundamentally *biological* processes,
the instincts.

However, Freud's texts and the supposed contradiction between instincts and instinctual representatives of which both
Strachey and Ricoeur accuse him[14] become much more intelligible
when we note that, according to Freud, repression is only one
among many possible vicissitudes an instinctual impulse may
undergo. That is, Freud's analysis of the relationship between
instinctual impulses and mental operations is essentially written from a developmental point of view.[15] More so, in "Instincts
and Their Vicissitudes," Freud never uses the term "instinctual
representative." On the contrary, he consistently describes the
biologically grounded, nearly automatic ways in which instinctual
impulses (or "instinctual stimuli") evolve, on their own, in the
earliest stages of human development.

> Love is derived from the capacity of the ego to satisfy
> some of its instinctual impulses [*Triebregungen*] auto-
> erotically by obtaining organ-pleasure. It is origi-
> nally narcissistic, then passes over on to objects,
> which have been incorporated into the extended ego.... [16]

The whole argument and point of view of the first essay is
biological, not psychological. Thus, Freud clearly states that
the ego is essentially biologically determined in this early
phase.

> The relation of the ego to the external world is pas-
> sive in so far as it receives stimuli from it and
> active when it reacts to these. It is forced by its
> instincts into a quite special degree of activity
> towards the external world, so that we might bring
> out the essential point if we say that the ego-
> subject is passive in respect of external stimuli
> but active through its own instincts. *The antithesis
> active-passive coalesces later with the antithesis
> masculine-feminine, which, until this has taken place,
> has no psychological meaning.*[17]

The whole argument and point of view of the second essay,
"Repression," is psychological. In it Freud laboriously
singles out repression as one among many possible vicissitudes
an instinctual impulse may undergo after a certain degree of
psychological development has taken place.

> Psycho-analytic observation of the transference
> neuroses, moreover, leads us to conclude that repres-
> sion is not a defensive mechanism which is present
> from the very beginning, and that it cannot arise
> until a sharp cleavage has occurred between conscious
> and unconscious mental activity....[18]

This sharp cleavage, about which we shall say more below, obviously entails the ability to distinguish self and world, inside and outside, and most importantly, to have some notion of
inner experience, that is, to be conscious of being conscious.
This obviously represents an immense step in psychological
development; most significantly for our discussion, it means
that the person (or his ego) can be conscious of instinctual
impulses. In Freud's language, the ego now recognizes the
ideational effects of the instincts. The instincts have a
representative (*Repräsentant*) which presents itself in consciousness as an idea (*Vorstellung*). In other words, repression
is a highly developed psychological process in which the ego
system rearranges the contents of its perceptions of the internal world in such a way that it can disown them.

Three Stages of Repression and the Return of the
Cathected Neurone

Freud maintains the distinction between "instinctual impulse" and "instinctual representative" in what would seem to
be two very similar discussions of the stages of repression.
In the Schreber analysis, he notes that the first phase of
repression

> ...consists in fixation, which is the precursor and
> necessary condition of every "repression." Fixation
> can be described in this way. One instinct or in-
> stinctual component fails to accompany the rest along
> the anticipated normal path of development....The
> libidinal current in question then behaves in rela-
> tion to later psychological structures like one be-
> longing to the system of the unconscious, like one
> that is repressed.[19]

In the essay on repression he says:

> We have reason to assume that there is a primal
> repression, a first phase of repression, which
> consists in the psychical (ideational) representa-
> tive of the instinct being denied entrance into the
> consciousness [der psychischen (Vorstellungs-)
> Repräsentanz].[20]

Again, the apparent contradiction between these two passages
can be resolved by noting that in the first Freud describes the
fundamental biological conditions, or dispositions of instinctual development that may be a source of danger or discomfort
for the ego, which is a "later psychological structure." In
the second passage he describes what happens when that structure is more or less completed and it confronts instinctual
derivatives (e.g., wishes and desires) which represent the on-
going demand made by the fixated libidinal trends. In other
words, contrary to what he says, Freud is describing two distinct steps in the development of repressive trends.

First Stage: fixation of a component instinct (e.g.,
                oral greed) occurs such that that in-
                stinct is not subordinated to genital
                sexuality at a phase specific time.

Second Stage: ideational representations of that
                fixated instinct (e.g., a wish to swal-
                low father's penis) approach conscious-
                ness but are denied entrance into
                consciousness = primal repression.

As the ego matures and the primally repressed ideas (and
the affects attached to them) continue their struggle for recognition, a third stage of repression comes about which Freud
terms, in both texts, "repression proper." This kind of repression is more highly developed, and seeks to repel or disown
derivatives of the repressed representatives.[21] It is this
form of repression one most often sees in neurotic behaviors,
e.g., parapraxes. A patient blocks or resists associations to
a seemingly innocuous idea because, Freud says, his ego senses
an imminent danger that the idea in question will unleash primally repressed wishes, desires, or fears. Because these
wishes and desires were primally repressed, they have not been
integrated into the personality; consequently,

> ...the instinctual representative develops with less
> interference and more profusely if it is withdrawn
> by repression from conscious influence. It prolifer-
> ates in the dark, as it were, and takes on extreme
> forms of expression, which when they are translated
> [via analysis] and presented to the neurotic...frighten
> him by giving him the picture of an extraordinary and
> dangerous strength of instinct.[22]

The crucial question then is, how does the ego effect this
third phase of repression? Freud gives a two-part answer. In
the essay on repression, he reverts to a clinical-descriptive
analysis of what he, the physician, observes in his patient's
behaviors. This description essentially repeats his discussion
of the attraction of the repressed, which as we have already
seen above, is based upon the even earlier concept of the
ability of cathected neurones to attract free-flowing cathexis
to themselves and so bind it.

> Repression proper...is actually an after-pressure.
> Moreover, it is a mistake to emphasize only the re-
> pulsion which operates from the direction of the
> conscious upon what is to be repressed; quite as
> important is the attraction exercised by what is
> primally repressed upon everything with which it
> can establish a connection. Probably the trend
> toward repression would fail in its purpose if
> these two forces did not cooperate....[23]

In "The Unconscious," he attempts to provide an economic
explanation of this attraction which relies upon the topographical theory of *The Interpretation of Dreams*. However, before

discussing that essay, it may be useful to describe more fully
the nature of the inner world to which Freud alludes in all the
essays.

The Intrapsychic Sphere and the Ego's Mutual Relations

If I am correct in distinguishing three stages of repression, instead of two as Freud and most of his commentators hold,
it is possible to more adequately distinguish the intrapsychic
sphere from both the nonpsychic somatic forces which affect it
from the inside and the nonpsychic reality forces which affect
it from the outside. To do this it will be clearer if we examine Freud's analysis of the former relationship and then
compare that to what we have already said about the latter.

While Freud does discuss the relationship of the ego to
the outer world in the last section of "The Unconscious," his
discussion of the same relationship in his monograph *On Aphasia*
more adequately displays his thinking and special way in which
he uses the two central terms, "idea" (*Vorstellung*) and "image"
(*Bild*). In the section of that work with which we are concerned,[24] Freud aims to explain various forms of speech disturbance from a functional, descriptive angle only, keeping "...the
psychological and anatomical sides of the question as separate
as possible."[25]

In order to do this, he adopts the rather standard empiri-
cist theory of the English philosophical tradition which, beginning with Locke, explains our perception and knowledge of
things in the world as a function of sense data organized in
the mental apparatus as "ideas."[26] Thus Freud posits that our
"ideas" (*Vorstellung*) or "presentations," as Strachey translates
the German, both of things in the world and words are complex
associations of simpler sense data or "images" (*Bild*).

> From the point of view of psychology the unit of the
> function of speech is the "word," a complex presenta-
> tion which proves to be a combination put together
> from auditory, visual and kinaesthetic elements. Four
> components of the word-presentation are usually dis-
> tinguished: the "sound-image," the "visual letter-
> image," the "motor speech-image" and the "motor
> writing-image."[27]

Granted this supposition, Freud can then go on and give an
associational theory of meaning; "A word...acquires its *meaning*
by being linked to an 'object-presentation,' at all events if
we restrict ourselves to a consideration of substantives."[28]
The object-presentation is, like the word-presentation, a complex of associations of various sense data linked by temporal-
spatial proximity. Hence, Freud concludes, learning to use
language, in any form, requires one to forge associational
links between the word- and object-presentations.[29]

     We can now combine this theory of perception and meaning-
attribution with our description of the three stages of repression and so produce a composite diagram of the mind which is
implied in the metapsychological papers.

BODY   ———————————————   EXTERNAL WORLD
(somatic processes)   "images" (*Bild*)
instinctual impulses   instinct representa-
                             tives   objects
                             "ideas" (*Vorstellung*)

                                   MIND
                             ———————————————

     Having assumed this "antiphenomenological" stance (Ricoeur),
Freud can then proceed to explain both somatically-based illnesses (e.g., anxiety neuroses) and illnesses which seem to be
a function of interpersonal relationships, e.g. melancholia.
Clearly, both kinds of illness will be played out within the
confines of the mental apparatus where the "ideas" or "representations" (*Vorstellungen*) of sexual urges and significant
persons interact. More importantly, from this point of view,
Freud can now explain why verbal therapy such as psychoanalysis
works; it works because judicious therapeutic intervention into
the patient's thought processes, that is, his mental functioning, will serve to rearrange poorly integrated "representations."[30]

     This general intrapsychic point of view did not, of course,
appear for the first time in the papers on metapsychology. In
his early work with hysterics, Freud hypothesized the significant mechanisms to be primarily intrapsychic (hysterics suffer
from reminiscences) and that treatment required certain

alterations of those memories. On the contrary, the metapsychological papers introduced two significant theoretical
advances. First, Freud enriched the libido theory by the addition of the fundamental notion of narcissism. Second, he am-
plified his theory of the intrapsychic agency which could criticize the ego and which, with its own more or less autonomous
energy store, could even punish it. He advanced both these notions in his great paper, "Mourning and Melancholia." However,
if we bracket the major questions of the nature of narcissism
and the superego, we see that Freud's major goal was to document the ego's response to reality demands that contradict its
emotional (libidinal) attachments. The arena of this conflict
is, again, the mental apparatus and *Vorstellungen* of significant persons and ideals are the central contestants. Thus
Freud explains the work of mourning.

> Reality-testing has shown that the loved object no
> longer exists, and it proceeds to demand that all
> libido shall be withdrawn from its attachments to
> that object. This demand arouses understandable
> opposition....This opposition can be so intense that
> a turning away from reality takes place and a cling-
> ing to the object through the medium of hallucinatory
> wishful psychosis. Normally, respect for reality
> gains the day. Nevertheless its orders cannot be
> obeyed at once. They are carried out bit by bit....
> Each single one of the memories and expectations in
> which the libido is bound to the object is accom-
> plished in respect of it.[31]

He explains the work of melancholia in a similar way but with
the significant addition that "...melancholia contains something more than normal mourning. In melancholia the relation
to the object is no simple one; it is complicated by the conflict due to ambivalence."[32] Because of this ambivalence and
the fact that the ego has repressed its hatred for the object,
the struggle to maintain the object is matched by an (unconscious) desire to kill it, to reject it. Consequently, the
ego is not aware of the full-fledged struggle going on within
the mental apparatus.

> We see that the ego debases itself and rages against
> itself, and we understand as little as the patient
> what this can lead to and how it can change. We can
> more readily attribute such a function to the

unconscious part of the work....Just as mourning
impels the ego to give up the object by declaring
the object to be dead and offering the ego the in-
ducement of continuing to live, so does each struggle
of ambivalence loosen the fixation of the libido to
the object....[33]

I should like to ask two rather simple questions about the
work which Freud says both mourning and melancholia accomplish:
(1) Granted that the ego succeeds in detaching its attachment
to the idea or representation of the disappointing object, what
is the fate of that abandoned representation? (2) Why is the
initial act of reality-testing that informs the ego of the
absence of the object not sufficient to immediately effect the
detachment of libido? That is, why must the ego initiate the
exhausting repetitiousness which Freud says characterizes these
two afflictions? I should like to answer both questions by re-
examining the way in which Freud explained the more fundamental
notion of reality testing in the metapsychological essays. In
brief, I shall suggest that, contrary to the model of reality-
testing introduced in the "Project," the notion of reality-
testing in these papers rests upon the more basic theorem that
the organism must continuously and repetitiously evaluate both
its environment and its responses to it in order to discriminate between "inside" and "outside."

Repetition, Reality, and the Immortal Object[34]

As I suggested above in my discussion of the "Project,"
Freud struggled with explaining how, in terms of the
physicalist-reductionistic assumptions of his model, fundamentally quantitative processes could transmit indications of
quality. Indeed, this is a significant problem for, as he
stated in that text, consciousness itself is always consciousness of qualities.[35] Because the real world is made up of
quantitative fluctuations only, qualitative perceptions must be
functions of the mental apparatus itself. Thus the ego, or
whichever agency[36] is responsible for the institution of
reality-testing, must accomplish two things: (1) make use of
quantitative procedures to differentiate perceptions, and (2)
maintain these quantitatively-based records through time and
so provide a means of comparing new perceptions against them.

These are precisely the conclusions Freud reaches in "A
Metapsychological Supplement to the Theory of Dreams" where he
summarizes his earlier propositions in "Instincts and Their
Vicissitudes" and the even earlier essay, "Formulations on the
Two Principles of Mental Functioning."

> ...we ascribed to the still helpless organism a capa-
> city for making a first orientation in the world by
> means of its perceptions, distinguishing "external"
> and "internal" according to their relation to its
> muscular action. A perception which is made to dis-
> appear by an action is recognized as external, as
> reality; where such action makes no difference, the
> perception originates within the subject's own body--
> it is not real.[37]

As we have already learned, instincts are precisely those internal forces which give rise to "representations," and wishes
which one cannot use against the most primitive defense of all,
flight. Thus the individual finds himself in a predicament;
he must adapt both to a frequently hostile outer world and to
an equally unknown inner world where he is subject to "...the
often merciless claims of his instincts."[38] There are two general ways out of this predicament: regression and progression.
He can regress by giving up the struggle against the demands of
his instincts and the prohibitions of his environment by acting
out those scenarios and wishes which normal people confine to
their fantasies. Also, he can reject those parts of reality
which are most painful to him and more or less hallucinate a
more pleasing one.[39] Other forms of regression need not be as
dramatic as these. Rather, the full range of neuroses, which
always entail some impairment of reality testing, are open to
him, including the daily narcissistic regression which sleep
offers.[40]

There are fewer ways to progress. On the whole, progression requires one to (1) inhibit immediate discharge, to think
rather than act, and (2) to sample and test the validity of the
"ideas" (urges, perceptions, wishes, fantasies) which emerge
into consciousness.[41] These two functions are the essential
components of reality-testing which, in the metapsychological
papers, Freud ascribes to the system *Cs*.

> This function of orientating the individual in the
> world by discrimination between what is internal and
> what is external must now...be ascribed to the system
> *Cs.* (*Pcpt.*) alone. The *Cs.* must have at its disposal
> a motor innervation which determines whether the
> perception can be made to disappear or whether it
> proves resistant. Reality-testing need be nothing
> more than this contrivance.[42]

While most of Freud's formulations on reality-testing in the
1915 papers are compatible with those very laconic ones in the
1911 essay ("Two Principles"), they also show a significant
difference. In the earlier essay, which depends very much upon
formulations in *The Interpretation of Dreams*,[43] he says that
reality-testing requires that consciousness have the ability
to perceive *qualities*.[44]

As I have said, Freud continuously struggled with the task
of explaining how essentially quantitative processes in the real
world are finally perceived as qualitative events. By dropping
the assumption that sense-organs directly perceive qualities,
and reverting back to an essentially quantitative explanation
of reality-testing, he produced a theory which was more congruent with his basic scientific orientation (the six assumptions
mentioned above). He also drastically altered the ontological
status of the inner and outer worlds and, by stressing the importance of the motor-innervation test, very much elevated the
role repetition plays in the construction of those worlds.

By more carefully examining the implications of his new
formulations, we can answer the two questions I raised about
the work which he says mourning and melancholia accomplish. In
addition, by schematizing the development of reality-testing,
we can gain some insight into the development of the object and
object-relations which, as we have seen, are central to Freud's
analysis of mourning and melancholia.

We may distinguish five steps in the development of
reality-testing.

1. The perceptual apparatus senses the presence of
   intense stimulation.

2. In obedience to the pleasure-principle, it tries
   to reduce the amount of stimuli by the most primitive defense, flight. If flight is successful,
   the crisis is passed, and no further psychological
   work need be done.

3. If flight fails, more complex modes must be
developed: "...the psychical apparatus had to
decide to form a conception of the real circumstances in the external world and to endeavor to
make a real alteration in them. A new principle
of mental functioning was thus introduced: what
was presented in the mind was no longer what was
agreeable [e.g., hallucinations of prior satis-
factions], but what was real, even if it happened
to be disagreeable."[45]

4. To accomplish this goal, the organism develops
functions of attention, notation, and memory.[46]

5. Thus the organism develops a mind which is capable
of representing experiences as "ideas" [*Vorstellungen*] and it has to "...decide whether a
given idea [*Vorstellung*] was true or false...the
decision being determined by making comparisons
with the memory-traces of reality."[47]

We may draw a number of conclusions from this theory of
the genesis of reality-testing which are pertinent to our
inquiry.

1. The original ego is a "reality-ego," not a
"pleasure-ego." That is, in the 1915 papers,
Freud suggests that the ego's original task is
to discern inside from outside, not to gain
immediate discharge of instinctual demands.

2. The ego constructs its picture of the inner and
outer worlds on the basis of the pleasure-pain
(discharge vs. non-discharge) criterion, not on
the basis of indications of quality.[48]

3. Thus to ensure adaptation, the ego must acquire
and maintain an accurate store of "ideas" [*Vorstellungen*] and the capacity to compare new perceptions against them.

4. Hence, from the beginning, the ego's chief orientation is towards the store of its "ideas," not
toward the world, for "...instincts and not external stimuli are the true motive forces behind
the advances that have led to the nervous system,
with its unlimited capacities, to its present
level of development."[49]

We can now do two things: (1) we can explain why the work
which mourning and melancholia perform requires so much time to
be completed, and (2) we can map out the fate of those intrapsychic object-representations from which, Freud says, the ego
must detach itself.

(1) Because the ego constructs its picture of the outer
and inner worlds over a period of time by testing and then
cathecting perceptions, "ideas" which arise from internal and
external sources, it cannot immediately "correct" its internal
picture of the outer world of significant objects when one of
them disappears, for example, by dying. When that happens, it
must face its internal world and the representations of that
object to which it had attached its interest, love, and self-
regard (its sexual and narcissistic libido) and, as it were,
reassess the status those representations enjoy against the
fact that the external object is lost.

> Normally, respect for reality gains the day.
> Nevertheless its orders cannot be carried out at
> once. They are carried out bit by bit....Each
> single one of the memories and expectations in which
> the libido is bound to the object is brought up and
> hypercathected and detachment of the libido is
> accomplished in respect of it.[50]

In both cases, that is, in the construction of the object-
presentation through reality testing and the decathexis of the
object through the work of mourning (or melancholia), the ego
grudgingly obeys the reality principle which requires it to
"...strive for what is *useful* and guard itself against
damage."[51]

(2) Although the ego may, through the work of mourning,
succeed in relinquishing its libidinal ties to it, the object-
presentation as such does not disappear or cease to play a
significant role in the individual's psychological functioning.
On the contrary, we must suppose that the object-presentation
persists as long as the original memory processes and conse-
quent behaviors occasioned by it persist. In addition, we may
add three more reasons why, with regard to psychic reality,
object-presentations are immortal.

> 1. "There is no 'No' in primary-process ideation.
> Death as nonbeing is a variant of 'No,' and in
> this respect it cannot be conceived (Freud, *SE* 14
> [1957 (1915b)] 296-297). Thus, from the subject's
> standpoint, there can be no thoroughgoing object
> loss. Only the higher levels of function, those
> more or less dominated by the secondary process,
> recognize 'No,' death, and loss...."[52]

2. "...the self and objects differentiate out of
   fragmentary, fluid, and amorphous primary experience, both are 'given' or immanent in all
   experience. The self is defined in relation to
   objects and vice versa. The representation that
   one exists in the world of objects or object
   relations is inherent in psychological experience.
   Consequently, the primary attachment to objects
   may be regarded as being as basic and inviolable
   as that to the self."[53]

3. Adaptive, reality-oriented, maturation of the ego
   requires that it master and incorporate regulatory
   features of significant objects: "Preliminary
   stages of love [of external objects] emerge as
   provisional sexual aims while the sexual instincts
   are passing through their complicated development.
   As the first of these aims we recognize the phase
   of incorporating or devouring--a type of love
   which is consistent with abolishing the object's
   separate existence and which may therefore be
   described as ambivalent."[54]

As Schafer remarks,[55] Freud only worked out the full implications of this conclusion in the structural essays of the
twenties when he elaborated the scope and significance identification has for the development of the ego. Indeed, as we
have seen in the brief review of the 1915 papers, in them Freud
raised the central problems of adaptation, integration, reality-
testing, and internalization with which the older topographic
picture of the apparatus could not deal.[56] By 1919, he had
turned his attention away from his intensive study of the instincts and toward the intrapsychic institutions, particularly
the ego, which loomed larger and larger as the most significant
features of the mental appratus. With regard to our own inquiry, I believe that a careful reading of the structural essays will verify what we have already seen demonstrated in the
papers on metapsychology, namely, that repetitious (and I shall
argue "ritualized") sampling and comparing of experiences is
essential to the development of reality-testing and therefore
to the development of the ego itself.

NOTES

CHAPTER VI

[1]Jones, *Life and Work*, 2.208.

[2]Strachey, Editor's Introduction to "Papers on Metapsy-chology," by S. Freud, pp. 105-107 in *SE* 14 (London: Hogarth Press, 1957).

[3]The five papers are: "Instincts and Their Vicissitudes," "Repression," "The Unconscious," "A Metapsychological Supplement to the Theory of Dreams," and "Mourning and Melancholia."

[4]For a complete review of the various meanings and uses to which Freud put this term, see the article, "Metapsychology," pp. 19-26 in Nagera, *Metapsychology*.

[5]Freud, "Instincts and Their Vicissitudes," 117.

[6]Ibid., 119.

[7]I am following Ricoeur's analysis very closely (*Freud and Philosophy*, 117-124).

[8]Freud, "Psycho-Analytic Notes on an Autobiographical Account of a Case of Paranoia (Demential Paranoides)," *SE* 12 (1958 [1911c]) 3-82.

[9]J. Strachey, Editor's Note to "Instincts and Their Vicissitudes," by S. Freud, pp. 111-116 in *SE* 14 (London: Hogarth Press, 1957).

[10]Freud, "Instincts and Their Vicissitudes," 121-122; *GW* 10.214.

[11]Idem, "The Unconscious," 177; *GW* 10.275.

[12]Ricoeur, *Freud and Philosophy*, 116.

[13]Freud, "Repression," 147.

[14]Idem, "Instincts and Their Vicissitudes," 113; Ricoeur, *Freud and Philosophy*, 137.

[15]Freud, "Instincts and Their Vicissitudes," 131.

[16]Ibid., 138; *GW* 10.231.

[17]Freud, "Instincts and Their Vicissitudes," 134, my italics.

[18]Idem, "Repression," 147.

[19]Idem, "Notes on Paranoia," 67.

[20]Freud, "Repression," 148; *GW* 10.250.

[21]Idem, "Repression," 148-149; "Psycho-Analytic Notes," 67.

[22]Idem, "Repression," 149.

[23]Ibid., 148.

[24]Six pages which Strachey excerpted and appended to "The Unconscious" as Appendix C, *SE* 14.209-215.

[25]Ibid., 209.

[26]In the text, Freud refers to J. S. Mill's *A System of Logic* (London: John W. Parker, 1843) which clearly reiterates the Humean analysis of perception as can be seen in the quotations below.

[27]Freud, Appendix C to "The Unconscious," 210.

[28]Ibid., 213.

[29]This supposition then allows Freud to rather elegantly explain two orders of aphasia; a first order aphasia in which associations between elements in the word presentation are disturbed, and a second order aphasia in which the meaning link between the word and object presentations is disturbed (ibid., 214).

[30]In Parts III, IV, V and VI of "The Unconscious," Freud offers an elaborate economic explanation of how the *Cs.* and *Pcs.* systems might control, via repression and partial expression, instinctual representatives from the *Ucs.* Briefly, he proposes that the system *Cs.* has the ability to align an "anti-cathexis" against highly cathected presentations from the *Ucs.* and that this constitutes the basis of repression proper (ibid., 181).

[31]Freud, "Mourning and Melancholia," 244-245.

[32]Ibid., 256.

[33]Ibid., 257.

[34]I take this term from Schafer's very important chapter "The Fates of the Immortal Object" in his text on internalization; see Schafer, *Aspects of Internalization*, 220-236.

[35]Freud, "A Project for a Scientific Psychology," 308.

[36]The fact that Freud rather continuously changed the locus of the agency responsible for reality-testing during the first three periods of the development of the metapsychology indicates how problematic the concept was for him. Thus, as was noted above, in the "Project" itself he rearranged the location of the ω system, which transmits indications of reality, a number of

times (see ibid., 310, n.). Apparently the missing paper on
consciousness contained similar reflections (see Strachey's
footnote in "A Metapsychological Supplement to the Theory of
Dreams," 232, n. 2). Even as late as 1920 he ascribed reality-
testing to the ego ideal (*Group Psychology*, 114).

[37]Freud, "A Metapsychological Supplement to the Theory of
Dreams," 232. In this text, Freud refers back to the passage
in "Instincts and Their Vicissitudes" (119) which I have already quoted above. In addition, one can find similar statements in the "Project," Part I, Sec. 15, the paper "Negation,"
and in Chapter I of *Civilization and Its Discontents*.

[38]Idem, "A Metapsychological Supplement to the Theory of
Dreams," 232.

[39]Ibid., 233.

[40]Ibid., 233-234.

[41]Ibid., 221.

[42]Ibid., 233.

[43]Freud, *Interpretation of Dreams*, 617ff.

[44]Idem, "Formulations on the Two Principles," 220.

[45]Ibid., 219.

[46]Ibid., 220-221.

[47]Ibid., 221; *GW* 8.233.

[48]Of course one can say that pleasure and pain are "qualities" themselves, hence the basis of reality-testing is still
a qualitative one. But, Freud's fundamental definitions of
pain are behavioral and biologically-based descriptions of the
organism's automatic, nonconscious, reaction against intense
stimuli which, in animals that have no mind, cannot be perceived as qualities. Also cf., "...the instincts are all quali-
tatively alike and owe the effect they make only to the amount
of excitation they carry, or...to certain functions of that
quantity" ("Instincts and Their Vicissitudes," 123).

[49]Ibid., 120.

[50]Freud, "Mourning and Melancholia," 244-245.

[51]Idem, "Formulations on the Two Principles," 223.

[52]Schafer, *Aspects of Internalization*, 221.

[53]Ibid., 225.

[54]Freud, "Instincts and Their Vicissitudes," 138.

[55]Schafer, *Aspects of Internalization*, 227.

[56]I have no discussed this topic which is, of course, central to the metapsychological papers, especially "The Unconscious." Rather, I will summarize the main features of the topography (the theory of the systems *Cs.*, *Pcs.*, and *Ucs.*), when I examine the structural essays.

CHAPTER VII

THE FOURTH PERIOD--PAPERS ON EGO PSYCHOLOGY

In this, the last great period of the flowering of his genius, Freud set out to more systematically order and synthesize the complex strands of theory, clinical insights, and therapeutic principles which he had put forth in the earlier periods. Thus, in addition to formulating the comprehensive structural model of the mental apparatus (ego, id, superego) which more or less summarizes and replaces the topographical suppositions of the earlier periods and which thereafter branded this period of his work as "the structural period," Freud also revised the instinct theory of the 1915 papers and radically altered his notion of the source and nature of aggression.

Since he most fully knits together these two strands of theory in the major essay of the period, *The Ego and the Id*, I will concentrate my discussion upon that work in the last part of this chapter. In the first part I shall briefly document these major shifts as they appear in Freud's own texts. In the middle section I will discuss the notion most relevant to our inquiry into the metapsychology of ritual, namely, the status and independence of the fifth concept in our set, the notion of the inner and outer worlds. My argument, in brief, will be that just as he showed that reality-testing and mourning were essentially functions of repetitious "ritualized" behaviors, so too in this last period he shows that the ego itself is a structure that develops through and requires a sequence of ritualized interactions with the "inner world" of instincts and the "outer world" of loved or hated objects.

From Topography to Structure

As we have seen, beginning with the essays on hysteria, Freud always considered it a requirement for a scientific psychology of the neuroses (and mental life in general) that it recognize and explain the reality of unconscious mental processes. Thus Fenichel states, "In all neurotic symptoms something happens which the patient experiences as strange and

unintelligible."[1] Through his work with hysteric patients, his
own dream analysis, and the evidence of hypnotically-induced
symptoms, Freud established that such experiences were "strange
and unintelligible" to the patient precisely because he or she
was not consciously aware of the motives and desires which their
odd behavior expressed. It is this interesting fact and subsequent clinical discoveries, such as the effect of abreaction,
that are the subject matter of psychoanalytic theory.

In his 1915 paper, "The Unconscious," he explicitly formulated the topographic theory which he had employed already in
Chapter VII of *The Interpretation of Dreams* and which was founded upon the distinction between conscious and unconscious por-
tions of the mental apparatus.[2] He hypothesized that there
are two, spatially-distinct systems within the mental apparatus
which are the locations of conscious ideas: the *Cs.*, and those
which are unconscious (due either to repression from consciousness or lack of opportunity to enter consciousness), the *Ucs.*[3]

> With the first, or topographical hypothesis is bound
> up that of a topographical separation of the systems
> *Ucs.* and *Cs.* and also the possibility that an idea
> [*Vorstellung*] may exist simultaneously in two places
> in the mental apparatus--indeed, that if it is not
> inhibited by the censorship, it regularly advances
> from the one position [in the *Ucs.*] to the other [in
> the *Cs.*], possibly without losing its first location
> or registration.[4]

Thus, he continues, when the analyst communicates to his patient an idea that the latter must have repressed, and the patient does not recognize or own that idea, it must be that the
idea in question now exists in two distinct parts of the mental
apparatus.

> ...now the patient has in actual fact the same idea
> in two forms in different places in his mental appara-
> tus: first, he has the conscious memory of the audi-
> tory trace of the idea, conveyed in what we told him;
> and secondly, he also has--as we know for certain--
> the unconscious memory of his experiences as it was
> in its earlier form.[5]

Although he partly modifies this particular spatial analogy in
the last section of the essay, "Assessment of the Unconscious,"
he maintains it throughout this and other essays of that period.

Indeed it is a fundamental part of his theory of repression (it
occurs in the three transference neuroses: anxiety hysteria,
conversion hysteria, and obsessional neurosis) for in each we
see that "...repression is essentially a process affecting
ideas on the border between the systems *Ucs.* and *Pcs.* *(Cs.).*"[6]

In Part V of "The Unconscious," Freud draws together many
of the conclusions that he reached both about the nature of the
systems *Ucs.* and *Pcs.* in the essay itself and in earlier works,
especially *The Interpretation of Dreams*. By rearranging the
statements of Part V, we can summarily present the distinguishing features of both systems.

System Ucs.	*System Pcs. (Cs.)*[7]
Nucleus consists of wishful impulse (or instinctual representatives) (and "thing-presentations") which are exempt from mutual contradiction.	Nucleus consists of word-presentations which are linked with the thing-presentation having been hyper-cathected by the system *Cs.* (*SE* 14.202).
Primary process modes dominante.	Secondary process modes dominate.
Cathectic intensities are mobile = freely mobile energy that seeks immediate discharge.	Cathectic intensities are bound and energy is not mobile; thinking and judgment replace immediate discharge (action).
Processes occurring within the system are not ordered temporally and are unaffected by passage of time.	The *Pcs.* is time-oriented, past pains and future rewards are content and it controls memory.
Ucs. processes ignore external reality and obey the pleasure-principle.	*Pcs.* processes therefore obey the reality-principle and weigh reality considerations; it carries out reality-testing.
Discharge of *Ucs.* processes produces affect (rather than thought).	Discharge of *Pcs.* processes issue in thought.
There is no direct access to consciousness; must rely upon dreams and other distorted expressions.	Has access to and control over consciousness and motility from a "very early moment" in the development of the mind.

By maintaining this sharply defined dichotomy, Freud was
able to offer a precise and inclusive metapsychological definition of the central clinical concept, repression.

> The system *Ucs.* contains the thing-cathexes of the
> objects, the first and true object-cathexes; the
> system *Pcs.* comes about by this thing-presentation
> being hypercathected through being linked with the

word-presentations corresponding to it. It is these
hypercathexes, we may suppose, that bring about a
higher psychical organization and make it possible
for the primary processes to be succeeded by the
secondary process which is dominant in the *Pcs*. Now,
too, we are in a position to state precisely what it
is that repression denies to the rejected presentation [*Vorstellung*] in the transference neuroses: what
it denies to the presentation is translation into
words which shall remain attached to the object. A
presentation which is not put into words, or a psychical act which is not hypercathected, remains thereafter in the *Ucs*. in a state of repression.[8]

However, having labored to establish the validity and use-
fulness of this twofold division of the mental apparatus, Freud
immediately goes on to raise serious problems with the entire
argument for "study of the derivatives of the *Ucs*....completely
disappoint our expectations of a schematically clearcut distinction between the two psychical systems."[9] Indeed, he goes on to
say that psychic balance requires a great deal of interplay between the two (or three) systems, "...a total severance of the
two systems, is what above all characterizes a condition of
illness."[10] We may list, in fact, five good reasons which
Freud offers in this brief chapter as to why a topographic
theory based on access to consciousness cannot succeed.

1. There are derivatives in the *Ucs*. which have all
   the characteristics of secondary processes, "...they
   are highly organized, free from self-contradiction,
   [and] have made use of every acquisition of the
   system *Cs*. and would hardly be distinguished in our
   judgment from the formations of that system."[11]

2. Some derivatives of the *Pcs*. cannot gain access to
   consciousness: "Now it becomes probable that there
   is a censorship between the *Pcs*. and the *Cs*."[12]
   And, when derivatives of the *Ucs*. circumvent the
   Pcs. and attempt to enter *Cs*., they "...are repressed
   afresh at the new frontier of censorship, between
   the *Pcs*. and the *Cs*."[13]

3. "The content of the system *Pcs*. (or *Cs*.) is derived
   partly from instinctual life (through the medium
   of the *Ucs*.), and partly from perception."[14]

4. "...the attribute of being conscious, which is the
   only characteristic of the psychical processes that
   is directly presented to us, is in no way suited to
   serve as a criterion for the differentiation of
   systems....Observation has shown that much that
   shares the characteristics of the system *Pcs*. does
   not become conscious...."[15]

5. He goes on to state what will be the keynote of
   his reform of the topographic theory in *The Ego and
   the Id*: "The truth is that it is not only the
   psychically repressed that remains alien to consciousness, but also some of the impulses which
   dominate are ego--something, therefore, that forms
   the strongest functional antithesis to the
   repressed."[16]

Taken together, these five criticisms constitute a radical
critique of the topographic theory in two vital areas: (1) It
no longer sufficiently explains the central clinical fact of
repression, of how one's own behavior may become strange and
unintelligible to oneself; and (2) by ascribing unconscious,
primary process behaviors to the ego system, it drastically alters the independent, more or less rational stature of the ego.
As he writes in the first section of *The Ego and the Id*, Freud
recognized that these two factors effectively ruled out using
the topographic theory to explain the most fundamental psychoanalytic clinical observation, namely that neurosis is always a
matter of intrapsychic conflict between two *opposing* systems.[17]

The Evolution and Dissolution of the Inner World

Before examining the *The Ego and the Id* itself, it will be
useful to analyze two texts which come between it and the 1915
essays. In the first, *Group Psychology and the Analysis of the
Ego*, Freud elaborated upon many of the central points we have
already examined in his papers, "On Narcissism" and "Mourning
and Melancholia." I shall suggest, more specifically, that in
this work Freud portrays the ego as an essentially unstable
structure maintained only by complex ritualized modes of interaction with the body and external world. In the second, *Beyond
the Pleasure Principle*, he elaborates the theory of primal instincts which will reappear as Chapter IV of *The Ego and the Id*.[18]

Although Freud published *Group Psychology* in 1921, Strachey
tells us that he had worked out the essential argument in late
1919 and early 1920, hence, while it was published a full year
after *Beyond the Pleasure Principle*, the works were composed
around the same time.[19] While, as we have already seen, the
latter text is composed of very high-level speculations and
rarely descends to clinical or applied issues, the former is

primarily an exercise in applied psychoanalytic clinical theory.
In it Freud hoped to explain the behavior of groups (*les foules*)
in terms of the development of the individual in relationship
to the primary group, the family. After examining the theories
McDougall,[20] Trotter,[21] and Le Bon[22] himself put forth, Freud
ventures to suggest that love relationships "...constitute the
essence of the group mind."[23] For it is clear that groups are
held together by some kind of power and "...to what power could
this feat be better ascribed than to Eros, which holds together
everything in the world?"[24]

Since, as he already had shown in the essay on narcissism,
the most primary love is narcissistic love or love for and pro-
tection of oneself, the love which binds groups together must
itself be a derivative of primary narcissism that somehow has
been arrested in its aim. In addition, on the basis of psychoanalytic clinical insight, Freud notes that there is an additional factor which serves to inhibit group solidarity, namely
a kind of primary aggression.

> The evidence of psycho-analysis shows that almost every
> intimate emotional relation between two people which
> lasts for some time--marriage, friendship, the rela-
> tions between parents and children--contain a sediment
> of feelings of aversion and hostility, which only es-
> capes perception as a result of repression.[25]

So, Freud concludes there is a twofold pressure against group
formation inherent in individual psychology, namely, the in-
stinctually-based drives of narcissism and primary aggressiveness. Because these two factors are fundamental to all psychic
functioning, group formation, or any other higher-level psychic
task, cannot succeed without allowing them at least indirect
expression. In other words, group formation and group psychology must represent vicissitudes, albeit high-level vicissitudes,
of the primary and indestructible instincts of eros and aggression. The process which accomplishes this amalgamation and
which constitutes the basis of group formation is identification.

In part seven of *Group Psychology*, "Identification," Freud
distinguishes the well-known phases which make up the development of object relations. In briefly recapitulating those
states, I should like to emphasize that, in Freud's description,

each higher stage is inherently less stable than that below it
and that even in the highest stage, where object relationships
are perfectly internalized in the form of the ego ideal, the
danger of structural regression persists. The four identifi-
able stages which Freud describes follow.

(1) *Introjection*[26]--This process, which is a derivative of
the earliest orally-based mode of taking in significant objects
via sucking (or punishing them by biting), is the most primitive
mode of internalization. It accomplishes the goal of keeping
the external object but only as an alien, nonself entity within
the intrapsychic sphere. Thus, as Freud had already pointed
out in his analysis of melancholia, the ego (which includes the
self as intrapsychic content) may actually punish that part of
the self-system which contains the introject.

> Analyses have shown that this disparagement and these
> reproaches apply at bottom to the object and represent
> the ego's revenge upon it. The shadow of the object
> has fallen upon the ego, as I have said elsewhere
> ["Mourning and Melancholia"]. The introjection of
> the object is here unmistakably clear.[27]

(2) *Identification*--In this second stage, which originally
occurs in the pre-oedipal to early-oedipal period, the significant object, for example, the boy's father, is internalized
both as "the person whom I shall be" and as "the way I am."[28]
In this stage, the internalized object representation is amal-
gamated with self-representations such that regulating and
controlling functions which the external object had upon the
child are now taken over by the child; the child learns "self-
control" and therefore acquires a higher degree of autonomy
over instinctual impulses which threaten its hard-won accord
between inner drives and outer restrictions.

(3) *Object-Love*--In this third stage, which may begin at
the same time as that of identification, "...the boy has begun
to develop a true object-cathexis towards his mother according
to the attachment type."[29] That is, he wants the external object, his mother, as an object with which he can gain sexual
pleasure. He does not want to *be* his mother, he wants to *have*
her. If the converse should occur, Freud says, one sees the

beginnings of a homosexual orientation in which the father is
sought as the love-object and the mother becomes the object of
the boy's identification. Object-love, however, is an especially unstable condition, kernels of animosity and aggressiveness which are inherent in all relationships, or the threat of
retaliation from other persons for one's object affections,
e.g., oedipally-based affections can subvert object-love into
identification.[30]

(4) *The Formation of the Ego Ideal*--Following the estab-
lishment of the capacity for object-love, the child develops
what Freud termed an ego ideal. It constitutes, in brief, both
a fully internalized representation of "the way one wants to
be" (which is, of course, a function of the teachings of external objects and the various strands of libidinal strivings) and
an intrapsychic agency, endowed with the ego's original share
of narcissim, which can criticize the ego (self) and repress
ideas arising from the unconscious.[31] Many, though not all, of
the attributes Freud ascribes to the ego ideal are secondary
process functions; it is able to compare past and present per-
formances with future possibilities (hence it has a well-
developed sense of time), it censors dreams and other primary
process-tinged productions and, as mentioned above, Freud even
ascribes reality-testing to it.[32]

Specifically, we can now say how the ego ideal regulates
the set of identifications which make up much of the ego's
character, and how, in turn, it serves to regulate the person's
object-relationships. It does the former by comparing and con-
trasting the present set of identifications, that is, representations of one's self which are "this is what I am," with a
second set derived from "...the most various models"[33] which express "this is what I should be." Because it has access to the
ego's original store of narcissistic libido, the ego ideal can
withhold it and so deprive the latter structure of its natural
satisfaction. Thus the ego ideal has the power to reinforce
behaviors which approximate those cathected as ideal representations and to punish (by withholding feelings of pride,
satisfaction, etc.) those behaviors which violate ideal

representations or which, in Erikson's terms,[34] approximate the negative ego ideal.

The ego ideal can regulate object relationships in those extreme circumstances, such as violent romantic love, hypnosis, and the formation of certain groups in which

> ...the object is...treated in the same way as our own ego [self], so that...a considerable amount of narcissistic libido overflows on to the object. It is even obvious, in many forms of love-choice, that the object serves as a substitute for some unattained ego ideal of our own. We love it on account of the perfections which we have striven to reach for our own ego [self], and which we should now like to procure in this roundabout way as a means of satisfying our narcissism.[35]

Thus the ego ideal regulates certain intense object-relations by replacing it with an internal relationship between ego and eto ideal such that directives and wishes of the external object, the person or group, can assume sufficient authority and intensity to override narrow, "selfish" ego interests. "The whole situation can be completely summarized in a formula: *The object has been put in the place of the ego ideal.*"[36] Having established this point, Freud goes on to immediately suggest that this is the fundamental mechanism that underlies the formation of primary groups.[37]

To recapitulate: Freud distinguishes four related phases of the development of object relations: Introjection--Identification--Object-Love--Formation of Ego Ideal. This is an essentially epigenetic conception of phase-specific processes, hence, poorly accomplished resolutions of oedipal identifications, for example, will necessarily lead to inadequate or poorly defined object relations, and those in turn will impair the development of integrated and realistic ego ideals. More so, based on the model of instinctual regression which he had observed in neurotic, psychosexual functioning, Freud implies that intense internal or external pressures brought to bear on a mature personality, such as severe disappointment in an idealized love relationship, will provoke some degree of regression.[38]

The severity of such regression will obviously be a function of the severity of the trauma and the adequacy of

identifications and other regulative features of the personality (ego strength). And, to return to our initial remarks on
the new, dual instinct theory he assumes in this text, it is
clear that all advanced psychic structures, even primitive
identifications, are finally no more than sophisticated vicissitudes of the primary instincts, eros and aggression. This
inescapable fact and unavoidable origin means, as we have already said, that all intimate emotional relationships are ambivalent, for they rest upon a foundation of love and hate.

But, even more tragic perhaps is the conclusion to which
Freud finds himself ineluctably drawn.

> ...it is precisely those sexual impulsions [*Sexual-
> strebungen*] that are inhibited in their aims which
> achieve lasting ties between people. But this can
> easily be understood from the fact that they are
> not capable of complete satisfaction, while sexual
> impulsions which are inhibited in their aims suffer
> an extraordinary reduction through the discharge of
> energy....It is the fate of sensual love to become
> extinguished when it is satisfied....[39]

The same is true of group ties; should its members lose their
nearly magical belief in and affection for their leader or their
shared ideal, "the group vanishes in dust, like a Prince Rupert's
drop when its tail is broken off."[40]

To summarize: in order to adapt themselves to a hostile and
dangerous external environment and to satisfy the unending demands of the internal world of instincts, both individuals and
groups must create psychological structures which inhibit discharge and encourage, therefore, an increase in psychic tension.
But, because all such construction must use the primary instincts, eros and aggressiveness, which are inimical both to
each other and to drive inhibition, it is always subject to
dissolution. More so, because the primary instincts are fundamental and because the pressure (*Drang*) which they exert upon
all mental structures is unvarying and continuous, the organism
must evolve behaviors which prevent dissolution of its psychological structures or, at least, encourage restructuralization.

The Maintenance and Repair of Structures:
The Work of Culture

Because both simple and complex mental structures are subject to the universal tendency of mental life, indeed all life,
towards zero potential (Nirvana principle), it follows that the
more sophisticated the structure the more tension the organisms
in question must endure in order to maintain it.[41] Thus, Freud
says, each of us returns in sleep to that earliest stage of
self-sufficient narcissism and so avoids the tasks of relating
to objects. With the development of the ego and ego ideal, such
periodic regression is more difficult and, obviously, more dangerous for the individual. Hence societies generate their own
periodic excuses for high-level regression.[42]

In addition, Freud notes that the great culture institutions of Art and Religion provide similar maintenance functions.
Following the slaying of the primal father and the formation of
the group perhaps there was a talented individual who "in the
exigency of his longing [for his lost father]"[43] created a
story which recaptured the father in fantasy.

> He who did this was the first epic poet; and the ad-
> vance was achieved in his imagination. This poet dis-
> guised the truth with lies in accordance with his
> longing. He invented the heroic myth. The hero was
> man who by himself had slain the father--the father
> who still appeared in the myth as a totemic monster.
> Just as the father had been the boy's first ideal,
> so in the hero who aspires to the father's place the
> poet now created the first ego ideal.[44]

Because the hero-myth is so central to group psychology, representing as it does a disguised version of the true account of
the origins of culture, it naturally happens that the hero is
deified.[45] As might be expected, Freud repeats his standard
diatribe against the illusions of religion by noting that to
the extent religious institutions promote the formation of ego
ideals and prevent individual regression, they protect the individual against suffering a private neurosis.

> Even those who do not regret the disappearance of
> religious illusions from the civilized world of today
> will admit that so long as they were in force they
> offered those who were bound by them the most powerful
> protection against the danger of neurosis.[46]

The Status of the Ego in *The Ego and the Id*

In analyzing this text and its relationship to its prede-
cessors, it will be useful to first summarize the three major
shifts in theory which it entails and then to analyze its individual chapters. Those three major shifts follow.

(1) The older topographic division of the mind into the
systems *Pcs*. (*Cs*.) and *Ucs*., which were distinguished on the
criterion of availability to consciousness, was abandoned and
replaced by a new division of the mind into "ego" and "id"
which were distinguished on criteria, immediacy of discharge,
kind of energy employed, and the relationship to repression.
Thus, rather than derive neurosis from the conflict between the
conscious and unconscious parts of the mind, Freud found it
more parsimonious to derive such conflicts from an "...anti-
thesis between the coherent ego and the repressed which is
split off from it."[47]

(2) Freud mated the dual-instinct theory of *Beyond the
Pleasure Principle* with the tripartite structural division of
the mind. Because the id included the vital layers of the apparatus, while the ego (and superego) represented regulative
mechanisms, it was obvious that the primal instincts, eros and
destructiveness, belonged to it. The id is that part of the
mind which, as Freud quotes Georg Groddeck, "lives" what we
call out ego.[48]

(3) Freud hypothesized a third form of instinctual energy,
called neutralized (or desexualized) libido which could be used
by the ego to adjust or regulate cathectic currents within the
apparatus by swelling the forces of drives or drive impulses
which opposed those that threatened it.

> We have reckoned as though there existed in the mind--
> whether in the ego or the id--a displaceable energy,
> which, neutral in itself, can be added to a qualita-
> tively differentiated erotic or destructive impulse,
> and augment its total cathexis.[49]

I should now like to analyze each chapter of the text and,
as I do, focus on three questions: (1) What is the status of the
ego vis-à-vis the id? (2) What is the role of repetition in ego

formation? (3) What relationships do ego defenses have to each
other and to the two primal instincts?

Chapter I

Freud repeats the arguments he had put forth in "Note on
the Unconscious in Psycho-Analysis" and "The Unconscious" in
favor of the psychoanalytic notion of the unconscious. In addition, he adds the crowning blow to the topographic theory by
stating, as we have already seen, that the ego itself, even
though it is a coherent organization of mental processes[50] has
an unconscious part to it--"and Heaven knows how important a
part...."[51]

Chapter II

Here he recapitulates his hypotheses, which he had elaborated in "The Unconscious," that thought processes in the *Ucs*.
(he continues to use these abbreviations even though they contradict his explicit renunciation of them) employ or make use
of object-presentations solely, while *Pcs*. and *Cs*. thinking
makes use of word-presentations in conjunction with object-
presentations.

However, he adds a significant conclusion, namely, that
there are two ways by which nonconscious materials (feelings and
ideas) can become conscious. (1) Ideas and thoughts, that is,
representations of objects, which have never been verbalized can
become conscious by associating themselves with memory traces of
once-conscious experience (i.e., *Pcs*. elements). Thus, when the
analyst recognizes that his patient is struggling to comprehend
pre-verbal experiences (and traumata), it is his task to offer
the latter interpretations which supply *Pcs*. links to the never-
before conscious materials.[52] (2) Excessive tensions within the
apparatus (which, of course, contradict the whole trend of mental life and which therefore create pressure towards discharge)
can become conscious as painful sensations by exciting the systems *Pcpt*. They do this by attaching themselves to the
pleasure-unpleasure series which is "...a something in the
course of mental events...."[53] Thus, "Even when they are not

attached to word-presentations, their becoming conscious is not
due to that circumstance, but they become so directly."[54]

Following this central distinction, Freud then goes on to
list some of the ego's major attributes, especially those which
distinguish it from the id.[55] The ego is:

--a coherent organization of mental processes.[56]

--a source of resistances and repression.[57]

--"...the entity which starts out from the system *Pcpt.*
and begins by being *Pcs*...."[58]

--"...that part of the id which has been modified by
the direct influence of the external world through
the medium of the *Pcpt.-Cs.*; in a sense it is an
extension of the surface-differentiation."[59]

--that agency which promotes the reality principle over
the pleasure principle, which controls access to
motility, and which "...represents what may be called
reason and common sense, in contrast to the id, which
contains the passions."[60]

--that agency which is most directly related to our
conception and idea [*Vorstellung*] of our body and
ourself.[61] Thus the ego is that agency or organization which is experienced as and dependent upon sub-
jective representations of one's body, hence it is
"...first and foremost a bodily ego...[it] is itself
a projection of a surface."[62] In more contemporary
language, the ego has a direct relationship to the
self.[63]

Finally, although the ego as agency is responsible for
self-control, resistances and repression of forbidden or dangerous impulses, and although it may, in so doing, represent a
kind of prudent common sense, it is not the agency responsible
for the highest degree of moral development. Rather the clinical reality of an "unconscious sense of guilt" suggests that,
"...not only what is lowest [e.g., infantile urges] but also
what is highest [the sense of guilt] in the ego can be
unconscious."[64]

Chapter III

Having ascertained the ego's functioning and mode of operation, Freud goes on to describe its ontogenetic and phylogenetic development. He slightly recasts the concept of identification, elaborates a theory of sublimation, correlates the new

theory of the ego with clinical theory of the oedipus complex,
and describes the origins of the superego which, we are told,
is a special modification of the ego and derived from oedipal
conflicts.

In place of the linear description of the development of
object-relations he had given in *Group Psychology* which, as we
have seen, says that object love develops out of identifications, Freud greatly complicates the picture by implying that
object-cathexis from the id is primary to identifications by
the ego.

> At the very beginning, in the individual's primitive
> oral phase, object-cathexis and identification are no
> doubt indistinguishable from each other. We can only
> suppose that later on object-cathexes proceed from
> the id, which feels erotic trends as needs. The ego,
> which to begin with is still feeble, becomes aware of
> the object-cathexes, and either acquiesces in them or
> tries to fend them off by the process of repression.[65]

In other words, in the very beginning of the development of the
personality, Freud hypothesizes that there is an ego-id matrix
in which the ego is not much more than the system *Pcpt.-Cs.*; it
has not yet attained autonomy. The id, on the other hand, is
more or less fully developed, since it represents the biologically given vital layer of the mental apparatus. Consequently,
it has control over or can influence the primitive ego systems
to gain its wishes, e.g., it cathects pleasure-giving objects
(or, perhaps, pleasure-giving wishes as in hallucination). But,
even in this early phase, it is clear that the ego has some independence and it can counteract the id's demands by repression,
that is, by subtracting attention cathexes which are energies
within its domain.

However, the match is quite unequal and, Freud conjectures,
the id can only be placated by the ego offering to replace the
lost object (e.g., mother's breast) by assuming the significant
features of that object itself.

> When it happens that a person has to give up a sexual
> object, there quite often ensues an alteration in his
> ego which can only be described as a setting up of the
> object inside the ego....It may be that this identifi-
> cation is the sole condition under which the id can
> give up its objects.[66]

In other words, the person may act like, eat like, or attempt
to look like the person or object which was lost and, at the
same time, he will consciously or unconsciously modify his
self-representations to reflect this change in character.[67]

The ego's willingness to suffer such transformations of
character and to acquiesce in the id's peremptory demands de-
creases as the organism develops; "...the effects of the first
identifications made in earliest childhood will be general and
lasting."[68] But because these first identifications are products of an early phase in which the ego's relationship to the
id is very much in favor of the latter agency, they are not
completely stable and well formed. So, when the intense sexual
yearnings of the early oedipal phase emerge in the phallic
stage, the id's demands are strengthened and the ego is faced
with the task of satisfying the id while safeguarding the organism as a whole.

And once again, the ego attempts to mediate between these
two demands through the mechanism of identification. However,
in contrast to the earliest periods, the increased libidinal
demands of the early oedipal period and the emergence of the
innate bisexuality of the sexual drive, make the ego's task
twice as difficult. It must satisfy not only the id's hetero-
sexual demands but its homosexual ones as well. A third com-
plication emerges when, as already mentioned, we realize that
all object relationships are ambivalent; that is, they are
themselves admixtures of the two primal instincts (Eros and
aggression) which emerge in psychological life as feelings of
love and hate.[69] So, the ego must, if it employs its usual
methods of identification, be ready to assume the features of
an object which is hated as well as loved. In economic terms,
it must be able to effectively channel large influxes of eros
and aggressiveness because

> closer study usually discloses the more complete
> Oedipus complex, which is twofold, positive and nega-
> tive, and is due to the bisexuality originally present
> in children: that is to say, a boy has not merely an
> ambivalent attitude towards his father and an affec-
> tionate object-choice towards his mother, but at the
> same time he also behaves like a girl and displays an
> affectionate feminine attitude to his father and a
> corresponding jealousy and hostility towards his
> mother.[70]

When the ego is faced with the task of ameliorating the inten-
sified feelings of love and hate for both parents which emerge
in the early oedipal period, it can only do so by identifying
with both parents and so satisfy the id's sexual and aggressive
demands while avoiding open confrontation with these more
powerful objects.

> The broad general outcome of the sexual phase dominated
> by the Oedipus complex may, therefore, be taken to be
> the forming of a precipitate in the ego, consisting of
> these two identifications in some way united with each
> other. This modification of the ego retains its spe-
> cial position; it confronts the other contents of the
> ego as an ego ideal or superego.[71]

So, by effecting this grand internalization, the ego is
able to satisfy the id, accommodate external reality, and most
importantly, resolve the oedipal crisis. However, this is not
an entirely happy solution for it is carried out by an "energetic reaction formation" against the original object-choices.
As we shall see in more detail below, a reaction formation is
an especially poor mode of ego defense because it simply pits
the ego and its allies against an instinctual derivative without defusing or altering the aim and intensity of the latter.
Indeed, reaction formation is an automatic and primary process
based response that creates poorly integrated behaviors and
attitudes which lack a depth basis and are not amenable to increased integration and differentiations. Therefore:

> ...the more powerful the Oedipus complex was and the
> more rapidly it succumbed to repression...the stricter
> will be the domination of the superego over the ego
> later on--in the form of conscience or perhaps of an
> unconscious sense of guilt.[72]

Having extricated itself out of the dangers of the full-fledged
oedipus complex through internalization, the ego once more finds
itself challenged and often controlled by the inescapable internal agent of the loved and hated parents.

> The way in which the superego came into being explains
> how it is that the early conflicts of the ego with the
> object-cathexes of the id can be continued in conflicts
> with its heir, the super-ego. If the ego has not suc-
> ceeded in properly mastering the Oedipus complex, the
> energetic cathexis of the latter, springing from the
> id, will come into operation once more in the reaction-
> formation of the ego ideal.[73]

The Status and Relationship of the
Superego to the Ego and the Id

Granted that the superego is born out of oedipal crises,
we must ask these three questions: (1) What is its status vis-
à-vis the two original agencies?   (2) Where does it get the
energies it needs to struggle against the ego and id?   (3)
Where does the ego get the energies it needs to struggle
against the superego?   The first question is answered in Chapter III, the last two in Chapter IV of *The Ego and the Id*.

It is clear that the superego is much more than a simple
reaction formation against intense oedipal desires.   For unlike
simple reaction formations which are rigid attitudes and habi-
tual patterns of instinctual denial generated by the ego, the
superego has the ability to confront and, at the same time,
punish the ego itself.   It can criticize the ego, withhold affection and praise from it, and in short, treat the ego and its
set of self-representations with the same authority that the
child's parents originally treated him.   More so, because of
its origins in the full-fledged oedipal crises, the superego is
partly endowed with the archaic drive-based motives of that
period; "By setting up this ego ideal, the ego has mastered the
Oedipus complex and at the same time placed itself in subject
to the id."[74]

To the extent that it controls archaic drive impulses
(both erotic and aggressive) which are discharged against the
ego, the superego represents the id.   But to the extent that it
carries out the teachings, prohibitions, and controlling functions of external authorities, it represents external reality
too.

> To the ego...living means the same as being loved--
> being loved by the super-ego, which here again appears
> as the representative of the id.   The super-ego ful-
> fills the same function of protecting and saving
> that was fulfilled in earlier days by the father and
> later by Providence of Destiny.[75]

Finally, to the extent that the superego is able to judge,
criticize, and compare the person's present status (his contemporary set of self-representations) with that which he hopes to
attain in the fugure, it manifests a secondary process time
sense and so represents the ego.

Because it may appear as the representative of so many
agencies and because it is a grade within the ego, Freud forth-
rightly avoids localizing the superego in the way he had the
ego and the id. More so, we ought to keep in mind that the
terms "ego," "id," and "superego" are high-level abstractions
which denote hypothetical psychological organizations, not
physical entities. In the well integrated person, we expect to
find that most of his psychological and physiological functions
mesh in such a way that no single internal organ system stands
apart from the others. Thus, it is only in crisis situations,
such as those that occur in the full-fledged oedipal complex,
that we can differentiate between ego and superego agencies.
Freud makes this point a number of times in *The Ego and the Id*
and in the following quotation he notes how closely connected
the three agencies are to one another.

> ...one must not take the difference between ego and id
> in too hard-and-fast a sense, nor forget that the ego
> is a specially differentiated part of the id. The
> experiences of the ego seem at first to be lost for
> inheritance; but, when they have been repeated often
> enough and with sufficient strength in many individuals
> in successive generations, they transform themselves
> so to say, into experiences of the id, the impressions
> of which are preserved by heredity...when the ego forms
> its super-ego out of the id, it may perhaps only be
> reviving shapes of former ego and be bringing them to
> resurrection.[76]

In this paragraph, we see Freud directly disavowing any
attempt to reify the ego, id, and superego agencies. On the
contrary, to say that the id may be "impressed" by repeated experiences, which must be mediated by the ego, and, that in turn
the superego is formed around the pattern of impressions of
those experiences, is to say that the id is a highly structured
agency that plays a central role in cultural and individual development. If one wished to remain faithful to a strictly
structural point of view which portrays the mind as divided up
between three rulings powers, one would have to say that the id,
in this example, is exhibiting a content and direction (preser-
vation of the self and the species) that is properly the domain
of the ego. However, the whole thrust of Freud's thinking in
the last period of the development of the metapsychology is away

from such rigid distinctions.[77] Rather, it seems he was concerned to portray the mind (mental apparatus) as a hierarchical
organization of functions which might conveniently be dissected
as ego, id, and superego agencies in terms of their distance
from and control over the organism's most fundamental impulses.

Chapter IV

In this chapter Freud attempts to correlate the new tripartite division of the mind with the dual instinct theory he
had introduced in *Beyond the Pleasure Principle*. Specifically,
he wishes to answer this question:

> ...whether the pleasure principle which dominates mental
> processes can be shown to have any constant relation
> both to the two classes of instincts and to these
> differentiations which we have drawn in the mind.[78]

Before outlining his answer, it will be helpful to follow
Bibring's[79] discussion of this text. Bibring points out that
Freud confounds the formerly distinct terms of "principle,"
"instinct," and "trend." As we have seen, in his earlier theory of instincts Freud carefully described them as quantities of
energy that arose from the organic functioning of the body and
which presented the mental apparatus with the demand for "work."
In contrast to the instincts, he described certain regulatory
principles by which the mental apparatus handled instinctual
demands; "...in this general view the instincts were not
thought of as directing the whole course of mental events, but
only as being sources of energy and causes of excitation which
set in motion the regulative trends of the mental apparatus."[80]
However, in the works of his last period, Freud completely altered his usage (while maintaining the same vocabulary) and he
attempted to generate a more holistic theory of mental functioning which would account both for fundamental biological
facts (e.g., organisms are born and die) and high-level psychological phenomena (e.g., repetition compulsion in certain neurotics, erotogenic masochism).

> The concepts of "instinct," "principle," "regulation,"
> thus seemed to be very much alike. Just as the in-
> stincts regulated the course of biological events, so,

> naturally, did they regulate the course of mental
> events. It was no longer possible to maintain a
> strict contrast between a mental apparatus regulated
> by principles and instincts pressing in upon it from
> the outside, since the instincts themselves now stood
> revealed as fundamental principles of life.[81]

Unless we keep this distinction firmly in mind, we will
find ourselves thoroughly confused by Freud when he says, for
example, that the id struggles against the libido.

> If it is true that Fechner's principle of constancy
> governs life, which thus consisted of a continuous
> descent towards death, it is the claims of Eros, of
> the sexual instincts, which, in the form of instinctual
> needs, hold up the falling level and introduce fresh
> tension. The id, guided by the pleasure principle...
> fends off these tensions in various ways.[82]

Clearly, in this passage, Freud implies that the id, as a part
of the mental mechanism, has the regulative task of keeping down
instinctual tension, in this case, the upsurge of libidinal
drives.[83] Obviously this portrait of the id as a regulative
agency working against the demands of libido is strikingly different from that more common one which shows it as a seething
cauldron of sexual impulses held in check only by a severe
superego.

The dual instinct theory is essentially a metabiological
theory grounded on the assumption that there are two fundamental trends in all life; one which aims at unification and crea-
tion of structures (Eros) and the other which aims at dissolution of structures (Destructiveness). Together they constitute
a theory which "...presupposes physiological processes running
in opposite directions."[84]

In addition to simplifying the earlier theories, amalgamat-
ing the structural theory and instinct theory allowed Freud to
partly account for the problem of quality which, as we have
seen, plagued him from the beginning. That is, by proposing
that the fundamental regulative trends of all life, including
mental life, are imbued with either erotic or aggressive qualities from the beginning, as it were, Freud could then rather
easily explain various manifestations of those instincts as
vicissitudes of their quantity alone. For example, he could now

deal with the complex problem of masochism by explaining it as
a manifestation of the naked destructive instinct inherent in
all life. More so, he could show a systematic parallel between
the vicissitudes of eros, which he had studied from the start,
and those of aggressiveness, which he had studied later. The
following chart, taken from Bibring's essay,[85] may make this
parallel obvious.

Life Instincts (Eros)	*Death Instincts* (Primal Sadism, Primal Masochism)
Sexual Instincts: Primary Narcissism Object Libido	Destructive Instincts: Primary Destructiveness Aggressiveness against the Object
Secondary Narcissism	Secondary Aggressiveness against the Self

Given that these are two primal, subpsychological instincts
endowed with innate qualities or aims, two questions arise: (1)
How do they combine or interact to make up the set of energies
that fuel psychological processes? (2) How does the mind, or a
special agency of it, counteract and more or less regulate their
naked power and their naked aims? Freud addresses himself to
both questions.

He answers the first by simply stating that we must assume
the two primal instincts are "fused, blended, and alloyed"[86]
with one another from the very beginning. As we ascend the
evolutionary scale we must assume that the organism develops
more and more sophisticated means of ridding itself of the
death instinct (overcoming the innate tendency towards tension-
less states). For example, we note that, while single-celled
creatures die as a result of their own life processes, multi-
celled organisms are able to discharge aggression via their
musculature against the external world "...and other
organisms."[87]

Finally, when we examine complex behaviors of organisms as
sophisticated as humans, in which a part of the external world
has been internalized as an additional control mechanism (e.g.,
the superego), we must assume that the two primal instincts
have been fused together. If this is so, then we can account

for the fact that many perversions, for example sadism, seem to
be regressions from more complex and integrated stages to lower
ones.

> Making a swift generalization, we might conjecture that
> the essence of a regression of libido (e.g., from the
> genital to the sadistic-anal phase) lies in a defusion
> of instincts, just as, conversely, the advance from the
> earlier phase to the definitive genital one would be
> conditioned by an accession of erotic components.[88]

As we shall see when we discuss the last chapter of this
text, Freud generalizes this principle to explain the superego's
murderous treatment of the ego, for "in suffering under the attacks of the superego...the ego is meeting with a fate like that
of the protista which are destroyed by the products of decomposition that they themselves have created."[89]

He answers the second question by referring back to his
earlier discussion of the process of internalization by which
the ego formed the ego ideal (superego). It is a fact established both by clinical observation and developmental observation that excessively intense and dangerous aggressive impulses,
for example, are often replaced by loving ones. Our entire discussion of the resolution of the Oedipus complex focused on the
proposition that the ego was able to counteract the id's erotic
cathexis of the mother and aggressive cathexis of the father by
means of reaction formation. But if this is so, then we must
conclude that the ego has access to neutralized energy with
which it can channel derivatives of the primal instincts.[90]

But how did the ego, which was, we are told, feeble and
ill-formed at its beginning, ever muster sufficient control to
tame the primal instincts and neutralize them for its own service? Freud's answer is brief but elegant: identification. As
he had already proposed in his discussion of the origins of the
superego, he stresses that, by identifying itself with an object
which is loved (or hated) by the id, the ego forces itself upon
the id and so receives the full brunt of the object cathexis
originally intended for the external object.[91]

Thus the neutral energy with which the ego checks and re-
directs the primal instincts is actually desexualized Eros.
While the semantic implications of this notion may appear to

damn it from the beginning, it is coherent and congruent with
the text's major thesis, namely, that structuralization requires
instinctual defusion. Furthermore, assuming it is desexualized
Eros which the ego uses, and as evidence of the correctness of
our assumption, we note two facts.

1. "[We] assume that this displaceable libido is
   employed in the service of the pleasure principle
   to obviate blockages and to facilitate discharge...
   it is easy to observe a certain indifference as to
   the path along which the discharge takes place, so
   long as it takes place somehow. We know this
   trait; it is characteristic of the cathectic processes in the id."[92]

2. "If this displaceable energy is desexualized libido,
   it may also be described as sublimated energy; for
   it would still retain the main purpose of Eros--
   that of uniting and binding--in so far as it helps
   towards establishing the unity, or tendency to unity,
   which is particularly characteristic of the ego."[93]

However, as is typical of his evaluation of the ego in
this text, Freud implies that desexualization endangers the ego
at the same time it provides it with necessary neutral energy
for

by thus getting hold of the libido from the object-
cathexes, setting itself up as sole love-object, and
desexualizing or sublimating the libido of the id, the
ego is working in opposition to the purposes of Eros
and placing itself at the service of the opposing
instinctual impulses [i.e., destructiveness].[94]

In fact, he grants the ego so little independence and autonomy
from the id he goes on to propose that his earlier ascription
of primal narcissism to it was wrong and that, in the beginning,
all libido is collected in the id. One may resolve the apparent
contradiction between the two texts by noting, as Strachey
does,[95] that Freud's underlying conception of the primal apparatus is that of an ego-id matrix in which all original libido
accumulates. However, this solution only highlights the ego's
dependency, weakness, and vulnerability in face of the much
older id and more powerful superego.

Chapter V ("The Dependent Relationships of the Ego")

In this last chapter, Freud attempts to diagram the developmental path which leads from a very weak ego menaced by the
threats of naked aggressiveness to that of a highly adapted
organ which "...develops from perceiving instincts to controlling them, from obeying instincts to inhibiting them."[96] However, it appears that the more cultured, refined, and moral a
man becomes towards others, the more severe and aggressive he
becomes towards himself. Why? Or, as Freud asks, "How is it
that the super-ego manifests itself essentially as a sense of
guilt...and moreover develops such extraordinary harshness and
severity towards the ego?"[97]

He answers by first rather briefly alluding to four varieties of superego punishment (which are experience of guilt)
that manifest different degrees of severity. Those four types
are, in order of their severity:

1. Normal, conscious sense of guilt--This is "...based
   on the tension between the ego and the ego ideal
   and is the expression of a condemnation of the ego
   by its critical agency."[98]

2. Guilt that occurs in obsessional neurosis--Here the
   person is conscious of intense guilt which seems
   out of proportion to his actual performance.
   "Analysis eventually shows that the super-ego is
   being influenced by processes that have remained
   unknown to the ego."[99] Thus the superego retali-
   ates against repressed impulses which are unknown
   to the ego.

3. Guilt that occurs, in a latent form, in hysteria--
   Here the person is conscious neither of the id
   impulses which threaten to emerge in action or
   consciousness nor of the superego's response to
   them. Thus the ego carries out a kind of double
   repression; it refuses to attend to the id's up-
   wellings and it fends off the superego's criticisms
   and threats.

4. Guilt that occurs in melancholia (depression)--Here
   the person is acutely aware of a sense of guilt
   which is out of all proportions to his real failings
   yet his ego "...brooks no objection; it admits its
   guilt and submits to the punishment."[100] As Freud
   had already shown in the early essay on melancholia,
   "...in melancholia the object to which the superego's wrath applies has been taken into the ego
   through identification."[101]

This last sentence contains the key with which Freud proposes
to unlock the mystery of the superego's sadism. He recalls his
earlier discussion of the mechanism of identification which, as
we have seen, is the means by which the ego overcomes the Oedipus complex. In economic terms, it appears that by internaliz-
ing the loved and hated object the ego also receives the brunt
of its object-cathexes. This in turn increases the ego's store
of neutral cathexes by desexualizing the primary instinct, Eros.
But this means that the total quality of sexualized, binding
Eros is diminished.

> After sublimation the erotic component no longer has
> the power to bind the whole of the destructiveness that
> was combined with it, and this is released in the form
> of an inclination to aggression and destruction. This
> defusion would be the source of the general character
> of harshness and cruelty exhibited by the ideal [super-
> ego]....102

It is difficult to overstate the ironic quality of Freud's portrait of the ego and, by extension, human culture. On the one
hand, in its early development it is tied to the id, it is a
"...submissive slave who courts his master's [the id's] love."103
On the other hand, in its highest state of moral and ethical
development, when the person has learned to curb his appetites,
to love others, and to do the work of culture, the ego must
suffer the pangs produced by criticisms from an often implacable
superego. Finally, as the agency responsible for reality-
testing, adaptation, and integration of competing biological and
cultural demands, the ego must respond to the demands, criticisms, and expectations of the external world as well.

> In its position midway between the id and reality, it
> only too often yields to the temptation to become
> sycophantic, opportunist and lying, like a politician
> who sees the truth but wants to keep his place in
> popular favor.104

Post-1923 Texts: The Advent of Ego Psychology

Following the composition of *The Ego and the Id*, Freud
attempted to consolidate major strands of the clinical theory,
especially the basic propositions about oedipal conflicts, both
with the new picture of the ego and the streamlined dual

instinct theory. In a series of short papers[105] he worked out
tentative formulations correlating neurosis and psychosis,
masochism, humor, fetishism, and therapeutic change with hypothetical alterations within the ego. Again and again one sees
Freud juggling formulations originally worked out in the context and language of topographic-instinct theory with the new
language and insights of the structural theory. For example,
in one of the early papers, "Neurosis and Psychosis," he explains neurosis as the result of conflict between the ego and
the id, psychosis as conflict between the ego and reality, and
melancholia (depression) as conflict between the ego and the
superego.[106]

Many of the papers, like "Analysis Terminable and Interminable," are especially noble expressions of Freud's willingness to admit his ignorance and challenge the sacred doctrines
of psychoanalytic theory. However, rather than discuss each of
them, I propose to summarize them and this section of this chapter on the metapsychology of ritual under the three following
rubrics: (1) The Ego's Role in Defense: The Cycle of Defenses;
(2) The Place of Adaptation: The Inner World; (3) Ego Formation
and Repetition: Repetition Compulsion as a Principle of Mental
Life.

The Ego's Role in Defense: The Cycle of Defenses

As we saw in our reading of *The Ego and the Id*, Freud
carefully avoided reifying the ego-id-superego agencies. On
the contrary, apart from clinical metaphors of their interaction, he consistently portrays them as way-points along a
developmental continuum which begins with an ego-id matrix and
extends to an ego-id-superego integrated set of functions.
The agencies are defined by their functions, distance from
immediate drive impulses, and degree of organization, not, as
one might suppose, by some anatomical boundary. Because this
is so, it follows that one ought not to isolate any single type
of behavior as uniquely an "ego function" or "id functioning."
Rather, as Rapaport continually stresses in his remarks on ego
development,[107] we should recognize that all behavior will
exemplify trends and features of all three agencies.[108]

Freud had already demonstrated this as early as 1926 when
he attempted to consolidate his thinking on the ego's role in
symptom formation.   In *Inhibitions, Symptoms and Anxiety* he
notes that we cannot distinguish ego, id, or superego functioning in a healthy person; "...if the ego remains bound up with
the id and indistinguishable from it, then it displays its
strength."[109] We can distinguish between the three agencies
only when severe conflicts arise between a less organized motive (e.g., an id "impulse") and a more organized layer of the
apparatus (e.g., ego inhibitions, or superego restrictions).
If the impulse does not gain direct access to motility and hence
hence discharge, a state of repression ensues. Freud warns
against picturing this circumstance as if "...the ego and the
id were two opposing camps...."[110] Rather, it appears that the
loosely organized impulse (e.g., an oedipally-based wish to
eliminate one's father) is isolated from the remaining mental
contents, achieves a degree of organization as it attracts
derivatives and, after perhaps years of slow construction, it
returns as a set of behaviors that make up a full-fledged
symptom.   Because symptoms are compromise formations, the ego
cannot fully resolve the underlying conflict, hence one sees an
"...interminable sequel in which the struggle against the instinctual impulse is prolonged into a struggle against the
symptom."[111]

But, again, the struggle against the symptom is not a
struggle between two antagonistic forces which are equally
matched and equally sophisticated. Rather the struggle is between disorganized and potentially disorganizing impulses and
the organism's need for regulated interaction with the social
environment and regulated satisfaction of its vital needs. As
the organ most responsible for effecting such regulation, the
ego attempts to negotiate a compromise between the competing
demands of the inner world and outer world by integrating the
trends of each into its character.

> It is therefore only natural that the ego should try to
> prevent symptoms from remaining isolated and alien by
> using every possible method to bind them to itself in
> one way or another, and to incorporate them into its
> organization by means of those bonds. As we know, a
> tendency of this kind is already operative in the very
> act of forming a symptom.[112]

When he replaced the topographic theory with the structural hypotheses, and so granted that the ego organization might
have unconscious aspects and operations, Freud effectively reduced the status of repression from that of the chief means of
instinct control to that of one mode of ego defense. If availability to consciousness was not the significant distinction
between the regulated and regulatory systems, then that process,
repression, which denied access to consciousness could not be
the universal defensive process Freud thought it was (e.g., in
the papers on metapsychology).

In *Inhibitions, Symptoms and Anxiety* Freud recognized these
conclusions and in a special addenda to that work, explicitly
stated that he wished to consider repression to be a subset of
ego defense in general.[113] The implications of this reformula-
tion are perhaps greater than they might at first appear to be.
That is, while it is true that he resurrected his very early
term "defence" (*Abwehr*) in the post-1923 essays, he did not also
resurrect his earlier, rather optimistic, opinions regarding the
possibility of eliminating or even preventing defense-neuroses.
On the contrary, he is much more pessimistic about the ego's
ability to overthrow, or empty out, the "unconscious." The
most famous text in which he expresses these dark doubts is, of
course, "Analysis Terminable and Interminable." Before turning
to that work, however, we may conclude these remarks on the
ego's defensive functioning by noting that according to the
structural essays, the ego is inextricably tied up with both
primary impulses (id impulses) and primary process functioning
(archaic forms of defense, e.g., denial). The conclusion is
inescapable; the more the ego attempts to integrate disorganized
impulses the more it takes on the characteristics of those impulses and in turn, the more it adapts to its now modified character, the more it must involve ever more sophisticated modes of
explaining itself to itself and to the sometimes perfectionistic
demands of others. Thus by its very nature, the ego is involved
in a cycle of defenses which it creates and cannot escape.

This cycle of defenses begins, as we have seen, in the act
of primal repression which is essentially an automatic ego-based
inhibition of immediate discharge that occurs unconsciously and

pre-verbally. It terminates in any of the thousand varieties
of conscious defenses. In a fully developed personality, in
which one can expect to find a loving as well as punishing
superego, conscious renunciation of the forbidden or dangerous
instinct may actually yield pleasure; one feels proud and of
good moral standing.

The Place of Adaptation: The Inner World

     Because of its special position between the id, that is
the vital layer of the mental apparatus, and the external world
with which it has intercourse via the systems *Pcpt.-Cs.*, the ego
has at least two distinct frontiers at which it must maintain
good relations. If we add to this constellation a well-formed
superego, we see that the ego must negotiate open borders, as
it were, with three distinct and sometimes conflicting powers,
the id, superego, and real world. If we further maintain a
strictly intrapsychic point of view, which is invariably en-
tailed by structural considerations, it follows that the ego
carries out its work of adaptation, organization, and fitting
together within the boundaries of the inner world.[114] Because
the ego is only a part of the mental apparatus, and not identical with the person, it can only modify or affect those psychological contents and functions over which it has control. Thus
the complex developmental processes of adaptation, whether to a
threatening external or internal danger, begin in the world of
fantasy.[115]

     Because the real world is ultimately painful, because
human life is grounded upon a series of frustrations which
necessarily hinder one's ability to enjoy living fully, and
because life itself leads us toward death, the ego can never
attend to reality absolutely.

          ...if the perception of reality entails unpleasure,
          the perception--that is, the truth--must be sacrificed.
          Where external dangers are concerned, the individual
          can help himself for some time by flight...until he is
          strong enough later on to remove the threat by actively
          altering reality. But one cannot flee from oneself;
          flight is no help against internal dangers. And for
          that reason the defensive mechanisms of the ego are
          condemned to falsify one's internal perception and to

give one only an imperfect and distorted picture of
one's id. In its relations to the id, therefore, the
ego is paralysed by its restrictions or blinded by
its errors....[116]

We may draw two rather disparate conclusions from this melan-
choly portrait of the ego. The first is that which Freud makes
the central theme of "Analysis Terminable and Interminable,"
namely, that the ego can never wholly shake off its dependence
upon the id and therefore everyone, including the most successful patients, Freud's pupils, must recognize the need for unending self-analysis and even periodical re-analysis.[117]

Second, granted that adaptation takes place within the
inner world, it follows that those teachings, such as religious
education, which produce an especially rich set of self and
object representations that populate the inner world may promote adaptation. Freud clearly considers this to be a central
feature in the formation of neurotic behavior, which is by
definition maladaptive.

Ego Formation and Repetition: Repetition Compulsion as a
Principle of Mental Life

We may conclude this long chapter and our recapitulation
of Freud's metapsychology of ritualized behaviors by summarizing what I believe are his most central conclusions regarding
the origin and maintenance of the ego. In brief, I shall suggest that, in the works of this last period, Freud unswervingly
concludes that the ego, the most precious organ of individual
and group survival, both creates and is created by repetitious
behaviors. We may discuss this claim under four broad
categories.

First, as we have already seen, in his last important
paper on technique, "Analysis Terminable and Interminable,"
Freud rather dramatically concludes that the ego and healthy
ego functioning require periodic renewal through the intense
regression which re-analysis requires.

Second, having postulated the existence of two fundamental
instincts which are absolutely antagonistic to one another, he
could not help but conclude that full resolution was impossible

and hence no single structure could long endure: On the contrary, we must follow the teachings of Empedocles

> ...who thought of the process of the universe as a
> continuous, never-ceasing alternation of periods, in
> which the one or the other of the two fundamental
> forces gain the upper hand, so that at one time love
> and at another strife puts its purpose completely
> into effect and dominates the universe, after which
> the other, vanquished, side asserts itself and in its
> turn defeats its partner.[118]

Third, the ego naturally tends toward unifying disparate
elements in the psyche, even if those elements are originally
hostile to one another. As we have seen, Freud says the ego
performs this mediating, organizing function by absorbing into
itself the originally conflicting trends, e.g., an id impulse
and a superego prohibition. Thus the ego can turn an originally
isolated symptom into a more or less esteemed part of the self.

> ...symptom-formation scores a triumph if it succeeds
> in combining the prohibition with satisfaction so that
> what was originally a defensive command or prohibition
> acquires the significance of a satisfaction as well....
> Such an achievement demonstrates the tendency of the
> ego to synthesize....[119]

Fourth, speaking at the most abstract level, because all
energies unrelentingly strive toward discharge, those structures, such as the ego, which seek to control them by inhibiting
direct discharge must themselves respond to those repetitious
demands by repetitiously binding them. We may document this
principle by recalling Freud's most fundamental proposition regarding bound and unbound energy. In the "Project" he clearly
intended to show that his portrait of the cathected neurone
could serve as an adequate model for all psychic structuralization. As I have suggested above, it is the cathected neurones'
ability to attract free-flowing energy ("Qh") to themselves and
hence to bind them which accounts for the most primitive forms
of psychic structure.[120]

If we leap ahead to Freud's last major theoretic text,
Inhibitions, Symptoms and Anxiety, we find him restating this
rather bald theorem in much more sophisticated language. In a
rather pessimistic section of that text he notes that he had

not yet found a simple theory which explained the aetiology of
neuroses. He then recapitulates his own which, of course,
states that the source of neurotic behavior lies in the ego's
automatic repressive response to certain instinctual impulses.
But repression is not always successful; new impulses may
strengthen the drive pressure or, more likely, the ego finds
itself more and more inhibited as it attempts to repress apparently harmless impulses and actions which have an unconscious
resonance to the repressed (i.e., the repressed attracts formerly neutral impulses to itself). Because this occurs unconsciously, the person finds himself acting in unreasonable and
"meaningless" ways.

> The new impulse will run its course under an automatic
> influence--or, as I should prefer to say, under the
> influence of the compulsion to repeat. It will follow
> the same path as the earlier, repressed impulse, as
> though the danger situation that had been overcome
> still existed. The fixating factor in repression,
> then, is the unconscious id's compulsion to repeat--
> a compulsion which in normal circumstances is only
> done away with by the freely mobile functions of the
> ego.[121]

At this point it might appear that it is quite incorrect
of me to ascribe repetitive functioning to the ego since Freud
clearly says that the "repetition compulsion" resides in the
"unconscious id." However, I believe there are two significant
points in favor of my interpretation. (1) As we have seen
Freud say many times, it is quite wrong to picture the ego and
id as two opposing institutions. On the contrary, "ego" and
"id" are names for sets of functions which are in turn defined
by the degree of energy discharge and inhibition of discharge
which obtain. (2) As we have seen in our analysis of the
"Project," all the ego's institutions, including its stock of
"freely mobile energy," derive from the fundamental microstructure of the cathected neurone. Since this is also the
fundamental structure of primal repression and accounts for the
later phenomena of the attraction of the repressed, it seems
arbitrary to restrict the "compulsion to repeat" to the id. On
the contrary, all Freud's reasoning suggests that repetition
compulsion is a regulative principle of all psychic functioning,
especially ego defense.

Repetition compulsion should also be reckoned among
the regulative trends. It is a general regulative
principle and serves to bind energies, i.e., to bring
them from a state of "flow" to one of "rest." That
a regulative trend of this sort does exist seems beyond doubt. The way in which the ego works, too,
presupposes this possibility of binding, and of
arresting tensions...the repetition compulsion seems
to be a sine qua non of all the other regulative
trends.[122]

If I am correct in my reexamination of the development of
Freud's thinking about the role repetition plays in the construction of the ego, and if it is fair to say that repetition
compulsion is one of the general regulative principles of mental life, it follows that not all repetitive behaviors, including religious rituals, are necessarily psychopathological.

And if this is correct, then the way lies open to reexamine
the potentially adaptive nature of religious rituals from a
strictly Freudian point of view without, at the same time,
agreeing to his entirely negative valuation of them.

[1]O. Fenichel, *The Psychoanalytic Theory of Neurosis* (New York: Norton, 1945) 18.

[2]Gill, *Topography and Systems*.

[3]Freud, "The Unconscious," 174.

[4]Ibid., 175; *GW* 10.274.

[5]Freud, "The Unconscious," 175. "In anxiety hysteria, a first phase...is frequently overlooked....It consists in anxiety appearing without the subject knowing what he is afraid of. We must suppose that there was present in the *Ucs*. some love-impulse demanding to be transposed into the system *Pcs*.; but the cathexis directed to it from the latter system has drawn back from the [*Ucs*.] impulse...and the unconscious libidinal cathexis of the rejected idea has been discharge in the form of anxiety" (ibid., 182).
  "A great deal of what we have found in anxiety hysteria also holds good for the other two neuroses....In conversion hysteria the instinctual cathexis of the repressed idea is changed into innervation [of a physical organ]..." (ibid., 184).
  "As regards obsessional neurosis...it is here that the anti-cathexis from the system *Cs*. comes most noticeably into the fore-ground. It is this which, organized as a reaction-formation, brings about the first repression, and which is later the point at which the repressed idea breaks through" (ibid., 185).

[6]Ibid., 180.

[7]I am summarizing pp. 186-189 of "The Unconscious." How-ever, in doing so I am inadvertently forcing a kind of systema-tization which Freud avoided for he clearly oscillated between claiming that the systems *Cs*. and *Pcs*. were distinct and claim-ing they were aspects of a single system; see especially pp. 188-189. Gill (*Topography and Systems*, 29) notes that, in "The Unconscious" and "A Metapsychological Supplement," Freud verged on ascribing the very highest systemic status to the *Cs*. which explicitly contradicts the notion of consciousness as a recep-tor sense organ. Much of this obscurity is doubtlessly due to the fact that Freud never revealed the paper on consciousness which was to complement the one on unconsciousness; see "The Unconscious," 188, n. 1.

[8]Freud, "The Unconscious," 201-202; *GW* 10.300. Freud also attempted to use this basic topographical theorem regarding ob-ject and word cathexes to explain how the process of repression occurred in a variety of mental disturbances: "In dreams the withdrawal of cathexis (libido or interest) affects all systems equally; in the transference neuroses the *Pcs*. cathexis [i.e., word-cathexis] is withdrawn; in schizophrenia, the cathexis of

the *Ucs*. [i.e., object-cathexis]; in amentia, that of the *Cs*. [hypercathexis of attention]" ("A Metapsychological Supplement," 235).

[9] Freud, "The Unconscious," 190.

[10] Ibid., 194.

[11] Ibid., 190.

[12] Ibid., 191.

[13] Ibid., 193.

[14] Ibid., 194.

[15] Ibid., 192.

[16] Ibid., 192-193.

[17] Freud, *The Ego and the Id*, 17.

[18] I will discuss the new dual instinct theory of *Beyond the Pleasure Principle* more fully when I examine the way in which Freud, in *The Ego and the Id*, reassigned eros and aggressiveness. The crucial difference between the two accounts is not in the nature of the primal instincts but in their location; in the earlier work Freud assigned the death instincts to the ego, while in the later work he assigned both death instincts and life instincts to the newly described vital layer of the mind, the id (cf. Bibring, "The Development and Problems of the Theory of the Instincts," *International Journal of Psycho-Analysis* 22 [1941] 102-131, especially 104).

[19] See Strachey's notes to both texts: *Group Psychology and the Analysis of the Ego*, 67, and *Beyond the Pleasure Principle*, 3.

[20] W. McDougall, *The Group Mind* (Cambridge: University Press, 1920).

[21] W. Trotter, *Instincts of the Herd in Peace and War* (London: T. Fisher Unwin, 1916).

[22] G. Le Bon, *Psychologie des Foules* (Paris: F. Alcan, 1895); idem, *The Crowd: A Study of the Popular Mind* (London: T. F. Unwin, 1903).

[23] Freud, *Group Psychology*, 91.

[24] Ibid., 92.

[25] Ibid., 101.

[26] I am very much relying upon Schafer's fundamental text on identification (*Aspects of Internalization*) in this section of this chapter. Freud does not consistently distinguish

between the terms "ego" and "self" nor "internalization" as a generic name for all varieties of intrapsychic object relations and more specific kinds such as introjection and identification.

[27] Freud, *Group Psychology*, 109.

[28] Ibid., 105.

[29] Ibid.

[30] Ibid., 106-109. "...identification may come from the Oedipus complex; in that case it signifies a hostile desire on the girl's part to take her mother's place, and the symptom [developing her mother's affliction] expresses her object-love towards her father, and brings about a realization, under the influence of a sense of guilt, of her desire to take her mother's place..." (ibid., 106).

[31] Ibid., 109-110.

[32] Ibid., 115.

[33] Ibid., 129.

[34] E. Erikson, *Childhood and Society* (New York: Norton, 1950), 243.

[35] Freud, *Group Psychology*, 112-113.

[36] Ibid., 113.

[37] Ibid., 116. This accounts for both types of libidinal ties found in group psychology; the leader is loved because he occupies the role of one's own ego ideal and one loves the other group members to the extent that when they share the same identification with the ideal they share parts of themselves, e.g., members of a monastic order can be brothers *in* Christ (ibid., 115-116). Although Freud does not explicitly say so in this text, in *Totem and Taboo* he suggested that sublimated homosexual feelings among the brothers in the primal horde also served to create group bonds (*Totem and Taboo*, 144); see also Freud's footnote to *Totem and Taboo* in part 10 of *Group Psychology*, 124, n. 1.

[38] Freud, *Group Psychology*, 108-110, 131-132.

[39] Ibid., 115; *GW* 13.127.

[40] Freud, *Group Psychology*, 97.

[41] Ibid., 130.

[42] Ibid., 131.

[43] Ibid., 136.

[44] Ibid.

[45]Ibid., 137.

[46]Ibid., 142.

[47]Freud, *The Ego and the Id*, 17.

[48]Ibid., 23.

[49]Ibid., 44.

[50]Ibid., 17.

[51]Ibid., 18.

[52]Ibid., 21. Thus with regard to fantasy, day-dreaming, and dreams proper, in which preconscious thought forms predominate, "we learn that what becomes conscious...is as a rule only the concrete subject-matter of the thought, and that the relations between the various elements in this subject-matter...cannot be given visual expression. Thinking in pictures is, therefore, only a very incomplete form of becoming conscious" (ibid.).

[53]Ibid., 22. This is hardly an illuminating analysis of this central topic and it indicates, I suggest, Freud was still struggling with the problem of accounting for the nature of quality in terms of a quantitative theory.

[54]Ibid., 23.

[55]I am following the way in which Rapaport ("Seminars on Psychoanalytic Ego Psychology Held at the Western New England Institute for Psychoanalysis") presents *The Ego and the Id* in his fourth seminar, "The Structural Concepts of Ego and Superego," 113-152.

[56]Freud, *The Ego and the Id*, 17.

[57]Ibid.

[58]Ibid., 23.

[59]Ibid., 25.

[60]Ibid.

[61]Ibid., 25-26; *GW* 13.253-254.

[62]Freud, *The Ego and the Id*, 26.

[63]The distinction between these two entities, which was stated very early by H. Hartmann ("Comments on the Psychoanalytic Theory of the Ego," pp. 113-141 in *Essays on Ego Psychology* [New York: International Universities Press, 1964]), forms the first step in a coherent analysis of narcissism; see Kohut (*Analysis of the Self*, xv) and Schafer (*Aspects of Internalization*, 79-81). Both of the quotations from Freud appear in Rapaport ("Seminars on Psychoanalytic Ego Psychology," 123).

[64]Freud, *The Ego and the Id*, 27.

[65]Ibid., 29.

[66]Ibid.

[67]"Since then [since the 1915 paper on melancholia] we have come to understand that this kind of substitution has a great share in determining the form taken by the ego and that it makes an essential contribution towards building up what is called its 'character' [*Charakter*]" (ibid., 28; *GW* 13.257).
    "At any rate the process [of identification], especially in the early phases of development, is a very frequent one, and it makes it possible to suppose that the character [*Charakter*] of the ego is a precipitate of abandoned object-cathexes and that it contains the history of those object-choices" (Freud, *The Ego and the Id*, 29; *GW* 13.257).

[68]Freud, *The Ego and the Id*, 31.

[69]Freud offered various explanations for the presence of oedipal ambivalence; that it was due to feelings of rivalry, jealousy which is a function of one's homosexual yearnings (ibid., 33), and innate aggression against the loved object which is expressed in the symbolically aggressive act of eating= introjecting (ibid., 29). Also, see his discussion of primal aggression in Chapter IV, ibid., 42.

[70]Ibid., 33.

[71]Ibid., 34; italics in original.

[72]Ibid., 34-35.

[73]Ibid., 39.

[74]Ibid., 36.

[75]Ibid., 58.

[76]Ibid., 38.

[77]It is easy to read Freud as saying precisely the opposite; thus D. Yankelovich and W. Barrett (*Ego and Instinct: The Psychoanalytic View of Human Nature--Revised* [New York: Random House, 1970] 411-413) criticize Freud's emphasis upon structures and applaud post-Freudian authors who emphasize notions of hierarchy and integration. Psychoanalytically-trained psychologists such as Schafer (*Aspects of Internalization*), Rapaport ("Seminars on Psychoanalytic Ego Psychology"), and Gill (*Topography and Systems*) agree with this criticism but tend to allow that Freud's own texts, including *The Ego and the Id*, reflect what Yankelovich and Barrett find more readily in later authors. Also see Chapter III of *Inhibitions, Symptoms and Anxiety*, 97-100.

[78]Freud, *The Ego and the Id*, 42.

[79]Bibring, "Theory of the Instincts."

[80]Ibid., 126.

[81]Ibid., 128.

[82]Freud, *The Ego and the Id*, 46-47.

[83]Or again, he clearly portrays the id as counteracting the demands of the instincts in the last lines of this fourth chapter (of *The Ego and the Id*); "Finally, as we have seen, the ego, by sublimating some of the libido for itself and its purposes, assists the id in its *work of mastering the tensions*" (ibid., 47, italics mine).

[84]Ibid., 43.

[85]Bibring, "Theory of the Instincts."

[86]Freud, *The Ego and the Id*, 41.

[87]Ibid.

[88]Ibid., 42.

[89]Ibid., 57.

[90]Ibid., 44.

[91]Rapaport ("Seminars on Psychoanalytic Ego Psychology") puts the matter rather succinctly: "So it [identification] is a double-barrelled deal. On the one hand, it is a method for the id to give up objects and on the other hand it is a method for the ego to get capital" (135).

[92]Freud, *The Ego and the Id*, 45.

[93]Ibid.

[94]Ibid., 46.

[95]See "Appendix B, The Great Reservoir of Libido" (ibid., 63-66).

[96]Ibid., 55-56.

[97]Ibid., 53.

[98]Ibid., 51.

[99]Ibid.

[100]Ibid.

[101]Ibid.

[102]Ibid., 54-55.

[103]Ibid., 56.

[104]Ibid.

[105]We may divide them into two broad categories; one comprises additions and modifications of psychoanalytic metapsychology, the other comprises reflections on and modifications of psychoanalytic technique. The first includes "The Infantile Genital Organization," *SE* 19 (1961 [1923e]) 141-145; "Neurosis and Psychosis," 149-153; "The Dissolution of the Oedipus Complex," *SE* 19 (1961 [1924d]) 173-179; "The Loss of Reality in Neurosis and Psychosis," 183-187; *Inhibitions, Symptoms and Anxiety*, 77-174; "Humor," 159-166; "Fetishism," *SE* 21 (1969 [1927e]) 149-157; *New Introductory Lectures on Psycho-Analysis*, *SE* 22 (1964 [1933a]) 3-182. The second includes "The Economic Problem of Masochism," 157-170; "Negation," 235-239; "Analysis Terminable and Interminable," 211-253; "Constructions in Analysis," *SE* 23 (1964 [1937d]) 257-269; "Splitting of the Ego in the Process of Defence," *SE* 23 (1964 [1940e]) 273-278.

[106]Freud, *The Ego and the Id*, 152-153.

[107]Rapaport, "Seminars on Psychoanalytic Ego Psychology."

[108]R. Waelder, "The Principle of Multiple Function," *Psychoanalytic Quarterly* 5 (1936) 45-62.

[109]Freud, *Inhibitions, Symptoms and Anxiety*, 97.

[110]Ibid.

[111]Ibid., 98.

[112]Ibid.

[113]Ibid., 164.

[114]Ibid., 98.

[115]Freud, "The Loss of Reality," 187.

[116]Idem, "Analysis Terminable and Interminable," 237.

[117]Ibid., 249.

[118]Ibid., 246.

[119]Freud, *Inhibitions, Symptoms and Anxiety*, 112.

[120]Gill (*Topography and Systems*) suggests that these minimal structures be called "microstructures" to distinguish them from the complex organizations of id, ego, and superego which might be termed "macrostructures" (8). He also quotes Glover's proposition that the most basic mental structure of all is the memory trace (cf. E. Glover, *Basic Mental Concepts* [London: Imago Press, 1947] 1). This analysis of the microstructure of the cathected neurone is also basic to Rapaport's posthumous paper on attention cathexis in which he makes this proposition: "...if an excitation (internal or external) attracts cathexis in a sufficient amount, for a sufficient length of time or with sufficient frequency, a structure is formed which may be either what is called a memory trace of an idea, or a relationship between ideas, or a structure of a threshold character (for instance, a defensive structure)," quoted by Gill and Klein, p. 28 in Rapaport, *The Collected Papers of David Rapaport.*

[121]Freud, *Inhibitions, Symptoms and Anxiety*, 153.

[122]Bibring, "Theory of the Instincts," 127, n. 4.

CHAPTER VIII

SUMMARY CONCLUSIONS:
THE ADAPTIVE CONSEQUENCES OF RITUALIZATION

In this last chapter I should like to summarize the arguments of the preceding chapters, and to distinguish the narrow psychoanalytic theory of ritual I have proposed from a general psychoanalytic theory of learning.

I began this work by noting that, contrary to what Freud and others thought he said about the psychopathological nature of religious ritual, there is no metapsychological argument in any Freudian text which explicitly demonstrates the supposed identity between religious behaviors and obsessive actions. Indeed, after reviewing the 1907 essay on that topic, I suggested Freud's actual statements imply that religious rituals are, generally, founded upon the nonpathological defense he termed "suppression" (*Unterdrückung*) rather than upon the frequently pathogenic defense he termed "repression" (*Verdrängung*).

After discussing the ways in which he used those two terms in his metapsychological texts, I concluded that while both are ego-oriented, anti-instinctual responses, they differ in significant ways.

Repression is a dynamically unconscious process, involves intrapsychic conflict, and always depletes the ego by binding upwardly directed, highly cathected, instinctual impulses with a "repressing current." Suppression is dynamically conscious, usually involves interpersonal conflict, and need not cause ego depletion. Because suppression takes place within the purview of consciousness, the ego is free to choose among alternative actions which can help it avoid or reduce interpersonal conflict yet also offer drive satisfaction.

Thus I argued, contrary to his rhetorical and personal dislike of religion and religious actions, Freud's metapsychological discussion in the 1907 essay suggests that rituals might, to the degree that they aid the ego's attempt to suppress disruptive or dangerous id impulses, further the cause of adaptation.

In the second chapter I tried to show how, in his later
texts on religion, Freud compounded his misreading of the metapsychological structure of religious rituals. By reinforcing
the rhetoric and forgetting the logic of the 1907 essay and by
using a weak clinical model of obsessional neurosis as a strong
model of religious behavior, he wove a too-biased and too-
unbelievable account of the original, primeaval event which,
according to the strong model, must underlie contemporary compulsions called religious rituals.

I concluded Chapter II by summarizing my major criticisms
of Freud's misuse of his own science and I suggested that one
could employ the immensely rich concepts of the metapsychology
to construct a low-level psychoanalytic theory of ritual. Before doing that I attempted to generate a working definition of
"ritual" which was amenable to psychoanalytic speculation but
did not immediately beg the question of its psychopathic and
prehistoric origins.

In Chapter III, I suggested that an adequate definition
of ritual would have to include the following five features:
human activity which is repetitive, function, symbolic, and
normative. I went on to examine Freud's *Beyond the Pleasure
Principle* with those definitional criteria in mind and with the
goal of correlating them with the fundamental metapsychological
concepts he uses in that very speculative essay. I proposed
that the following metapsychological concepts, taken from that
essay, most directly pertain to our neutral definition of
ritual; psychic pain, the pleasure-unpleasure series, primary
and secondary defense, repetition-hallucination, and inner and
outer reality.

In Chapters IV through VII, I analyzed the way in which
Freud developed each of these concepts in the various phases of
his theoretical works, beginning with the "Project" of 1895 and
ending with *An Outline of Psycho-Analysis* which was written in
1939. In my analysis I tried to show how, contrary to popular
belief, Freud never portrayed the ego, which is the most important part of the mental mechanism, as a static "structure" or
as a miniature personality hidden within the mind where it once
and for all instituted reality-testing, impulse control, memory,

etc. Rather I argued that Freud consistently portrayed the ego
and other structures of the mental mechanism as essentially
dynamic organizations of correlated functions distinguished by
their mode of discharge.

In other words, the hypothetical boundary between the ego
and the id is a function of the presence or absence of the
ability to control basic human drives, e.g., sex and aggression.
The more one can control, direct, and harmonize one's behavior
the larger is one's ego.

Once we grasp this central notion we see that one cannot
define the ego or any other hypothesized mental structure as a
forever fixed mental entity. On the contrary, as I have tried
to show in my discussion of reality-testing, we must recognize
that the ego itself is a product of ritualization and requires
ritualized behaviors to maintain itself. The boundaries between the various mental structures, whether we call them the
systems *Ucs.* and *Cs.* or ego and id, are only maintained by
repetitious reenactment of specific behaviors which are functional, symbol laden, and normative, e.g., sampling perceptions
which arise from external objects and comparing them against a
set of representations drawn from memory. In other words, the
ego requires and promotes ritual behaviors.

To use a metaphor, the ego can only maintain its fluid
boundaries with inner and outer reality by repetitiously push-
ing back the two waves of stimuli which come from the much
larger and more powerful external world and from the much more
mysterious inner world.

It might seem that I have put forth a general psychoanalytic theory of learning under the guise of a specific theory of
ritual since I so strenuously insist that ritualized behaviors
underlie the ego institution Freud named reality-testing. However, as I noted in Chapter III, it appears that human and
infrahuman ritual behaviors are more similar to what the
ethnologists can IRM's (Innate Releasing Mechanisms) than they
are to conditioned reflexes or to more advanced types of learning. Obviously persons in different cultures perform different
religious acts which we assume they learned within their specific

environments. But anthropological and ethnological studies
(e.g., Lorenz, Huxley, and Leach)[1] suggest that the sequence
ubiquity, and structural similarities of cross-species rituals
indicate that they all may be functions of a commonly shared,
unlearned, substrate. We noted that Leach went as far as to
suppose that there may be "ritemes" which, like morphemes and
phonemes in structural linguistics, are prebehavioral units of
significance that act as constituent units of more complex and
highly differentiated ritual actions.

In addition, the whole force of our reconstruction of the
metapsychology of ritual favors the proposition that ritualized
boundary maintenance is necessary for smooth ego functioning
which, in turn, is a prerequisite for advanced learning. That
is, if one defines learning as abiding behavioral change wrought
by experience[2] and, at the same time, defines ritual as essentially conservative and repetitive behavior, it follows that
ritualization by itself cannot constitute learning.

It was precisely the nonsensical, repetitious, conservative, and unchanging aspects of religious rituals which Freud
found most similar to the apparently meaningless neurotic rituals of his patients. Indeed, the person who suffers from obsessive compulsive symptoms cannot, without treatment, learn to
stop performing his rituals. This fact suggests that psychopathological ritualization preempts and then blocks high-level
learning processes.

We can explain this in terms of the theory of ego maintenance put forth in Chapter VII: if all higher level ego functions depend upon the ritualized cathexis and decathexis of
self and object representations, then severe distortion of that
boundary through an especially strong upsurge of instinctual
impulses, for example, would create a kind of primary defect in
ego functioning. It seems plausible to conclude that such primary defects could only be repaired by intensive ritualized
actions which we can see in many forms of neurotic and psychotic
restitutions and which certainly occur in ritualized treatments
such as psychoanalysis.[3]

Finally, while it is true that one learns a specific ritual
text or action, it also seems true that such rituals are founded

upon and may only be successful to the extent they exemplify
the unlearned substrate of needs, motivations, and thought
processes which constitute the id's heritage. To the extent
that the id is archaic, prestructural and unmodified by learning, we must conclude that ritual behaviors which directly or
indirectly reflect its operations are also archaic and unlearned.

Having more or less successfully argued these claims about
the minimum features of ritual behavior and the ritual formation
of the ego, the way lies open to reconsider a psychoanalytic
theory of religious ritual which fully reflects Freud's metapsychology without, at the same time, championing his theology.

NOTES

CHAPTER VIII

[1]Lorenz, *On Aggression*; Huxley, "Courtship-Habits";
Leach, "Ritual."

[2]As Rapaport, for example, did in his many papers on
structure formation, see Gill's introduction to *The Collected
Papers of David Rapaport* (27-29).

[3]This would also explain, in part, why nonanalytic and
indeed non-Western kinds of psychotherapy which employ complex
rituals can effect cures even though their practitioners lack
scientific training in depth psychology.

SELECTED BIBLIOGRAPHY

Works by Authors Other than Freud

Abel, K. *Über den Gegensinn der Urworte*. Leipzig:
W. Friedrich, 1884.

Abraham, K. *Traum und Mythus*. Leipzig: Deuticke, 1909.

_____. "Restrictions and Transformations of Scoptophilia in
Psycho-Neurotics." In *Selected Papers*. Trans. D. Bryan.
London: Hogarth Press, 1927.

Allport, Gordon. *The Use of Personal Documents in Psychological
Science*. New York: Social Science Research Council, 1942.

Amacher, Peter. *Freud's Neurological Education and Its Influence on Psychoanalytic Theory*. Psychological Issues 16.
New York: International Universities Press, 1965.

Arlow, J and Brenner, C. *Psychoanalytic Concepts and the
Structural Theory*. New York: International Universities
Press, 1964.

Austin, J. L. *How To Do Things With Words*. New York: Oxford
University, 1962.

Barros, Carlos P. "Thermodynamic and Evolutionary Concepts in
the Formal Structure of Freud's Metapsychology." Pp. 72-
111 in *World Biennial of Psychiatry and Psychotherapy*.
Ed. Silvano Arieti. New York: Basic Books, 1973.

Benedict, Ruth. "Ritual." Pp. 396-398 in *Encyclopaedia of the
Social Sciences* 13. Ed. E. R. A. Seligman. New York:
Macmillan, 1934.

Berger, Peter. *The Sacred Canopy: Elements of a Sociological
Theory of Religion*. New York: Doubleday, 1967.

Bernfeld, S. "Freud's Earliest Theories and the School of
Helmholtz." *Psychoanalytic Quarterly* 13 (1944) 341-362.

_____. "Sigmund Freud, M.D., 1882-1885." *International
Journal of Psycho-Analysis* 32 (1951) 204-217.

Bibring, E. "The Development and Problems of the Theory of the
Instincts." *International Journal of Psycho-Analysis* 22
(1941) 102-131.

Birdwhistell, Roy L. *Introduction to Kinesics: (An Annotation
System for Analysis of Body Motion and Gesture)*. Louisville: University of Louisville, 1952.

Boden, Margaret A. *Purposive Explanation in Psychology*.
Cambridge, MA: Harvard University, 1972.

Boring, E. G. *A History of Experimental Psychology*. 2nd ed.
New York: Appleton-Century-Crofts, 1950.

Bossard, James A. S. and Bell, Eleanor S. "Ritual in Family
Living." *American Sociological Review* 14 (1949) 463-469.

Brilliant, R. *Gesture and Rank in Roman Art*. Memoirs of the
Connecticut Academy of Arts and Sciences 14. New Haven:
The Academy, 1963.

Brown, Norman O. *Life Against Death*. Middletown, CT: Wesleyan
University, 1959.

Cardwell, Donald Stephen Lowell. *From Watt to Clausius; The
Rise of Thermodynamics in the Early Industrial Age*.
Ithaca, NY: Cornell University, 1971.

Coleridge, S. T. "Biographia Literaria." In *Coleridge:
Selected Poetry and Prose*. Ed. E. Schneider. New York:
Holt, Rinehart and Winston, 1965.

Davis, M. *Understanding Body Movement: An Annotated Bibliography*. New York: Arno, 1972.

Du Bois-Reymond, Emil H. *Untersuchungen über tierische Elek-
tricität*. Vol. 2. Berlin: G. Reimer, 1849.

Du Bois-Reymond, Estelle. *Jugendbriefe von Emil du Bois-Reymond
an Eduard Hallmann*. Berlin: G. Reimer, 1918.

_____. *Zwei grosse Naturforscher des 19. Jahrhunderts. Ein
Briefwechsel zwischen Emil Du Bois-Reymond und Karl
Ludwig*. Leipzig: J. A. Barth, 1927.

Durkheim, Émile. *The Elementary Forms of the Religious Life*.
London: Allen and Unwin, 1912. New York: Macmillan, 1954.

Eissler, K. Panel on "A Critical Assessment of the Future of
Psychoanalysis." *Journal of the American Psychoanalytic
Association* 23 (1975) 139-153.

Ellenberger, Henri F. *The Discovery of the Unconscious*.
New York: Basic Books, 1970.

Erikson, E. *Childhood and Society*. New York: W. W. Norton,
1950.

_____. *Childhood and Society*. 2nd ed. New York: W. W.
Norton, 1963.

_____. "The Ontogeny of Ritualization." In *Psychoanalysis--
A General Psychology*. Ed. Loewenstein et al. New York:
International Universities Press, 1966.

Evans-Pritchard, E. E. *Theories of Primitive Religion*.
Oxford: Oxford University, 1965.

Exner, S. *Entwurf zu einer physiologischen Erklärung der psychischen Erscheinungen.* Vienna: Deuticke, 1894.

Feldman, A. Bronson. "Freudian Theology." *Psychoanalysis: Journal of Psychoanalytic Psychology* 1/3 (1953) 31-52.

Fenichel, Otto. *The Psychoanalytic Theory of Neurosis.* New York: W. W. Norton, 1945.

Ferenczi, S. "A Little Chanticleer." In *First Contributions to Psycho-Analysis.* London: Hogarth Press, 1952.

Frazer, J. G. *Totemism and Exogamy.* 4 vols. London: Macmillan, 1910.

Freud, Anna. *The Ego and the Mechanisms of Defense.* Rev. ed. New York: International Universities Press, 1966.

_____. "Obsessional Neurosis: A Summary of Psycho-Analytic Views as Presented at the Congress." *International Journal of Psycho-Analysis* 47 (1966) 116-122.

Fromm, Erich. *Psychoanalysis and Faith.* New Haven: Yale University, 1950.

Frosch, J. "Psychoanalytic Considerations of the Psychotic Character." *Journal of the American Psychoanalytic Association* 18 (1970) 24-50.

Gay, V. P. "Psychopathology and Ritual: Freud's Essay 'Obsessive Actions and Religious Practises.'" *Psychoanalytic Review* 62 (1975) 493-507.

Gedo, John E. and Goldberg, Arnold. *Models of the Mind.* Chicago: University of Chicago, 1973.

Gill, Merton M. *Topography and Systems in Psychoanalytic Theory.* Psychological Issues 10. New York: International Universities Press, 1963.

Glick, B. S. "Freud, the Problem of Quality and the 'Secretory Neuron.'" *Psychoanalytic Quarterly* 35 (1966) 84-97.

_____. "A Note on Freud's 'Empty' Neuron." *British Journal of Medical Psychology* 40 (1967) 159-162.

Glover, E. *Basic Mental Concepts.* London: Imago, 1947.

Greenfield, N. S. and Lewis, W. C., eds. *Psychoanalysis and Current Biological Thought.* Madison: University of Wisconsin, 1965.

Greenson, R. R. *The Technique and Practise of Psychoanalysis.* New York: International Universities Press, 1967.

Groddeck, G. *Das Buch vom Es.* Vienna: Internationaler Psychoanalytischer Verlag, 1923.

Harrison, Jane. *Themis: A Study of the Social Origins of
    Greek Religion.* Cambridge: Cambridge University, 1912.

_____. *Ancient Art and Ritual.* London: Williams and
    Norgate, 1913.

Hartmann, Heinz. *Ego Psychology and the Problem of Adaptation.*
    New York: International Universities Press, 1961 (1939).

_____. "Comments on the Psychoanalytic Theory of the Ego."
    Pp. 113-141 in *Essays on Ego Psychology.* New York: Inter-
    national Universities Press, 1964.

_____. "Notes on the Theory of Sublimation." Pp. 215-240
    in *Essays on Ego Psychology.* New York: International
    Universities Press, 1964.

Hartmann, Heinz; Kris, E.; and Loewenstein, R. M. "Comments on
    the Formation of Psychic Structure." *Psychoanalytic Study
    of the Child* 2 (1946) 11-38.

_____. "Notes on the Theory of Aggression." *Psychoanalytic
    Study of the Child* 3/4 (1949) 9-36.

Holder, Alex. "The Genetic Point of View." Pp. 43-46 in *Basic
    Psychoanalytic Concepts on Metapsychology, Conflicts,
    Anxiety and Other Subjects.* Ed. Humberto Nagera. New
    York: Basic Books, 1970.

_____. "Cathexis." Pp. 77-96 in *Basic Psychoanalytic Con-
    cepts on Metapsychology, Conflicts, Anxiety and Other
    Subjects.* Ed. Humberto Nagera. New York: Basic Books,
    1970.

Hollis, M. "Reason and Ritual." Pp. 221-239 in *Rationality.*
    Ed. Brian Wilson. New York: Harper and Row, 1970.

Holt, Robert R. "A Critical Examination of Freud's Concept of
    Bound vs. Free Cathexis." *Journal of the American Psycho-
    analytic Association* 10 (1962) 475-525.

_____. "A Review of Some of Freud's Biological Assumptions
    and Their Influence on His Theories." Pp. 93-124 in
    Psychoanalysis and Current Biological Thought. Ed. N. S.
    Greenfield and W. C. Lewis. Madison: University of
    Wisconsin, 1965.

_____. "Freud's Mechanistic and Humanistic Images of Man."
    Psychoanalysis and Contemporary Science 1 (1972) 3-24.

Holzman, Philip S. *Psychoanalysis and Psychopathology.* New
    York: McGraw Hill, 1970.

Homans, Peter. *Theology After Freud: An Interpretive Inquiry.*
    New York: Bobbs-Merrill, 1970.

Home, J. "The Concept of Mind." *International Journal of Psycho-Analysis* 48 (1966) 42-49.

Hook, S., ed. *Psychoanalysis, Scientific Method, and Philosophy: A Symposium.* New York: Grove Press, 1959.

Huxley, J. S. "The Courtship-Habits of the Great Crested Grebe (Podiceps cristatus); with an Addition to the Theory of Sexual Selection." *Proceedings of the Zoological Society of London* 35 (1914) 491-562.

Isakower, O. "On the Exceptional Position of the Auditory Sphere." *International Journal of Psycho-Analysis* 20 (1939) 340-348.

_____. "Spoken Words in Dream: A Preliminary Communication." *Psychoanalytic Quarterly* 25 (1954) 6.

Jackson, J. Hughlings. "On Affections of Speech from Disease of the Brain." *Brain* 1 (1878) 304-330.

Jones, Ernest. *Papers on Psycho-Analysis.* London/New York: Baillier, Tindall and Cox, 1913.

_____. "The Madonna's Conception Through the Ear." Jahrbuch der Psychoanalyse, Band VI, 1914. Pp. 266-268 in *Essays in Applied Psycho-Analysis.* London: Hogarth Press, 1951.

_____. "The Theory of Symbolism." *British Journal of Psycho-Analysis* 9 (1916) 181. Pp. 87-144 in *Papers on Psycho-Analysis.* 5th ed. London: Bailliere, Tindall and Cox, 1948.

_____. "A Psycho-Analytic Study of the Holy Ghost Concept" (1922). Pp. 358-373 in *Essays in Applied Psycho-Analysis.* London: Hogarth Press, 1951.

_____. *The Life and Work of Sigmund Freud.* 3 vols. New York: Basic Books, 1953-1957.

Jung, C. G. *Wandlungen und Symbole der Libido.* Leipzig: Deuticke, 1912.

Kanzer, M. "The Transference Neurosis of the Rat Man." *Psychoanalytic Quarterly* 21 (1952) 181-189.

Kaufmann, Walter. *Goethe's Faust.* Garden City, NY: Anchor Books, Doubleday, 1961.

Kohut, Heinz. "Forms and Transformations of Narcissism." *Journal of the American Psychoanalytic Association* 14 (1966) 243-272.

_____. "The Psychoanalytic Treatment of Narcissistic Personality Disorders." *The Psychoanalytic Study of the Child* 23 (1968) 86-113.

Kohut, Heinz. *The Analysis of the Self.* New York: Inter-
    national Universities Press, 1971.

Kris, E. "The Significance of Freud's Earliest Discoveries."
    International Journal of Psycho-Analysis 31 (1950) 1-9.

_____. *Psychoanalytic Explorations in Art.* New York:
    International Universities Press, 1952.

Kroeber, A. "Seven Mohave Myths." *Anthropological Record* 11/1
    (1948).

Kubie, L. S. "Body Symbolism and the Development of Language."
    Psychoanalytic Quarterly 3 (1935) 430-444.

_____. "Instincts and Homeostatis." *Psychosomatic Medicine*
    10 (1948) 15-30.

_____. "The Central Representation of the Symbolic Process
    in Psychosomatic Disorders." *Psychosomatic Medicine* 15
    (1953) 1-7.

_____. "The Distortion of the Neurotic Process in Neurosis
    and Psychosis." *Journal of the American Psychoanalytic
    Association* 1 (1953) 59-86.

_____. "The Fundamental Nature of the Distinction Between
    Normality and Neurosis." *Psychoanalytic Quarterly* 23
    (1954) 167-204.

_____. "Influence of Symbolic Processes on the Role of
    Instincts in Human Behavior." *Psychosomatic Medicine* 18
    (1956) 189-208.

_____. "The Neurotic Process as the Focus of Physiological
    and Psychoanalytic Research." *British Journal of Psycho-
    Analysis* 104 (1958) 518-532.

Langs, R. J. *The Technique of Psychoanalytic Psychotherapy.*
    2 vols. New York: Jason Aronson, 1974.

Leach, E. R. "Ritual." Pp. 520-526 in *International Ency-
    clopedia of the Social Sciences* 13. Ed. D. L. Sills.
    New York: Macmillan, 1968.

Le Bon, G. *Psychologie des Foules.* Paris: F. Alcan, 1895.
    (*The Crowd: A Study of the Popular Mind.* London: T. F.
    Unwin, 1903.)

Levey, Harry B. "A Critique of the Theory of Sublimation."
    Psychiatry 2 (1939) 239-270.

Lévi-Strauss, Claude. "The Structural Study of Myth." Pp. 81-
    106 in *Myth: A Symposium.* Ed. T. Sebeok. Bloomington/
    London: Indiana University Press, 1958.

Lorenz, Konrad. *On Aggression.* Trans. M. Latzke. London:
     Methuen, 1966.

Lukes, S. "Some Problems About Rationality." Pp. 194-213 in
     Rationality. Ed. Brian Wilson. New York: Harper and
     Row, 1970.

_____. "Political Ritual and Social Integration."
     Sociology 9/2 (1975) 289-308.

McDougall, W. *The Group Mind.* Cambridge: The University
     Press, 1920.

Madison, Peter. *Freud's Concept of Repression and Defense.*
     Minneapolis: University of Minnesota, 1961.

Marcuse, H. *Eros and Civilization.* Boston: Beacon, 1955.

Menninger, Karl. *Theory of Psychoanalytic Technique.* New
     York: Basic Books, 1958.

Mill, J. S. *A System of Logic.* London: John W. Parker, 1843.

Miller, Ira. Reporter for Panel on "A Critical Assessment of
     the Future of Psychoanalysis: A View from Within." *Jour-
     nal of the American Psychoanalytic Association* 23 (1975)
     139-153.

Minsky, M. L. "Matter, Mind, and Models." Pp. 45-49 in *Pro-
     ceedings of the International Federation of Information
     Processing Congress.* Vol. 1. Washington, DC: Spartan,
     1965.

Mol, H. "The Sacralization of Identity." (Typewritten, 1975).
     Published as *Identity and the Sacred.* Oxford: Basil
     Blackwell, 1976; New York: Free Press, 1976.

Moxon, Cavendish. "A Psycho-Analytic Study of the Christian
     Creed." *International Journal of Psycho-Analysis* 2 (1921)
     54-64.

Myerson, P. "Comment on Dr. Zetzel's Paper." *International
     Journal of Psycho-Analysis* 47 (1966) 139-142.

Nagel, Ernest. "Methodological Issues in Psychoanalytic
     Theory." Pp. 38-56 in *Psychoanalysis, Scientific Method
     and Philosophy: A Symposium.* Ed. Sidney Hook. New York:
     New York University, 1959.

Nagera, Humberto, ed. *Basic Psychoanalytic Concepts of the
     Libido Theory.* Hampstead Clinic Psychoanalytic Library 1.
     New York: Basic Books, 1969.

_____. *Basic Psychoanalytic Concepts on the Theory of
     Dreams.* Hampstead Clinic Psychoanalytic Library 2. New
     York: Basic Books, 1969.

Nagera, Humberto, ed. *Basic Psychoanalytic Concepts on Meta-psychology, Conflicts, Anxiety and Other Subjects*. Hamp-stead Clinic Psychoanalytic Library 4. New York: Basic Books, 1970.

_____. *Basic Psychoanalytic Concepts on the Theory of Instincts*. Hampstead Clinic Psychoanalytic Library 3. New York: Basic Books, 1971.

Nagera, Humberto and Colonna, Alice. "Freud's Theory of Con-flict." Pp. 97-112 in *Basic Psychoanalytic Concepts on Metapsychology, Conflicts, Anxiety and Other Subjects*. Hampstead Clinic Psychoanalytic Library 4. Ed. Humberto Nagera. Basic Books, 1970.

Nuttin, J. "Human Motivation and Freud's Theory of Energy Discharge." *Canadian Journal of Psychology* 10 (1956) 167-178.

Parsons, Talcott. *The Structure of Social Action*. Glencoe: Free Press, 1949.

Peirce, C. S. "A Neglected Argument for the Reality of God." Pp. 358-380 in *Values in a Universe of Chance*. Ed. Philip P. Wiener. Stanford: Stanford University, 1958.

Philip, H. *Freud and Religious Belief*. London: Rockliff, 1956.

Posinsky, S. H. "Ritual, Neurotic and Social." *American Imago* 19 (1962) 375-390.

Pribram, K. "Freud's Project: An Open, Biologically Based Model for Psychoanalysis." Pp. 81-92 in *Psychoanalysis and Cur-rent Biological Thought*. Ed. Norman S. Greenfield and W. C. Lewis. Madison: University of Wisconsin, 1965.

Pruyser, P. *A Dynamic Psychology of Religion*. New York: Harper, 1968.

Radford, Pat. "Principles of Mental Functioning." In *Basic Psychoanalytic Concepts on Metapsychology, Conflicts, Anxiety and Other Subjects*. Ed. Humberto Nagera. New York: Basic Books, 1970.

Rank, Otto. *Der Mythus von der Geburt des Helden*. Leipzig/Vienna: Deuticke, 1909.

_____, and Sachs, H. *The Significance of Psychoanalysis for the Mental Sciences*. Trans. C. R. Payne. New York: Nervous and Mental Diseases, 1916.

Rapaport, David. "The Conceptual Model of Psychoanalysis." Pp. 405-431 in *The Collected Papers of David Rapaport*. Ed. Merton Gill. New York: Basic Books, 1967.

Rapaport, David. "Some Metapsychological Considerations Concerning Activity and Passivity." Pp. 530-568 in *The Collected Papers of David Rapaport*. Ed. Merton Gill. New York: Basic Books, 1967.

_____. *Organization and Pathology of Thought: Selected Sources*. New York: Columbia University, 1951.

_____. "Seminars on Psychoanalytic Ego Psychology Held at the Western New England Institute for Psychoanalysis." Ed. Stuart C. Miller. Typewritten, 1955.

_____. "Seminars on Elementary Metapsychology Held at the Western New England Institute for Psychoanalysis." 3 vols. Ed. Stuart C. Miller. Typewritten, 1957.

_____. "Seminars on Advanced Metapsychology Held at the Western New England Institute for Psychoanalysis." 4 vols. Ed. Stuart C. Miller. Typewritten, 1957.

_____. "The Theory of Ego Autonomy: A Generalization." Pp. 722-744 in *The Collected Papers of David Rapaport*. Ed. Merton Gill. New York: Basic Books, 1967.

_____. "On the Psychoanalytic Theory of Motivation." Pp. 853-916 in *The Collected Papers of David Rapaport*. Ed. Merton Gill. New York: Basic Books, 1967.

_____. *The Structure of Psychoanalytic Theory*. Psychological Issues 6. New York: International Universities Press, 1960.

_____. "The Theory of Attention Cathexis: An Economic and Structural Attempt at the Explanation of Cognitive Processes." Pp. 778-794 in *The Collected Papers of David Rapaport*. Ed. Merton Gill. New York: Basic Books, 1967.

_____. *The Collected Papers of David Rapaport*. Ed. Merton Gill. New York: Basic Books, 1967.

Reik, Theodor. *Ritual: Psychoanalytic Studies*. London: Hogarth Press, 1931.

_____. *Dogma and Compulsion: Psychoanalytic Studies of Religion and Myths*. New York: International Universities Press, 1951.

Ricoeur, Paul. *The Symbolism of Evil*. Boston: Beacon, 1967.

_____. *Freud and Philosophy*. New Haven: Yale University, 1970.

Rieff, Philip. *Freud: The Mind of the Moralist*. New York: Doubleday, 1959.

Roazen, Paul. *Freud: Political and Social Thought*. New York: Random House, 1968.

Roheim, G. "Psycho-Analysis of Primitive Culture Types."
    International Journal of Psycho-Analysis 13 (1932) 1-224.

_____. *Psychoanalysis and Anthropology*. New York: Inter-
    national Universities Press, 1950.

_____. *Magic and Schizophrenia*. Bloomington: Indiana
    University, 1955.

Schafer, 'Roy. "The Loving and Beloved Superego in Freud's
    Structural Theory." *Psychoanalytic Study of the Child* 15
    (1960) 163-188.

_____. *Aspects of Internalization*. New York: International
    Universities Press, 1968.

Scharfenberg, J. Lecture delivered to the Center for Religion
    and Psychotherapy of Chicago, February 13, 1975.

Schur, Max. *The Id and the Regulatory Principles of Mental
    Functioning*. New York: International Universities Press,
    1966.

Scientific American 228. 28 February 1973. "The Paranoid
    Computer." Pp. 48-49.

Shakow, David and Rapaport, David. *The Influence of Freud on
    American Psychology*. New York: International Universities
    Press, 1964.

Silberer, H. *Problems of Mysticism and Its Symbolism*. New
    York: Moffat, Yard and Co., 1917.

Simon, H. A. *The Sciences of the Artificial*. Cambridge: MIT,
    1969.

Skinner, B. F. "Critique of Psychoanalytic Concepts and
    Theories." *Scientific Monthly* 79 (1954) 300-305.

Sperber, Dan. *Le Symbolisme en Général*. Paris: Hermann, 1964.

Spitz, René A. *No and Yes: On the Genesis of Human Communica-
    tion*. New York: International Universities Press, 1957.

_____. "Aggression and Adaptation." *Journal of Nervous
    and Mental Diseases* 149 (1969) 81-90.

Strachey, J. Editor's Introduction to "Inhibitions, Symptoms
    and Anxiety," by S. Freud. Pp. 77-86 in *Standard Edition*
    20. London: Hogarth Press, 1959.

_____. "The Emergence of Freud's Fundamental Hypotheses."
    Pp. 62-68 in *Standard Edition* 3. London: Hogarth Press,
    1962.

Strachey, J. Editor's Introduction to "Papers on Metapsychol-
    ogy," by S. Freud. Pp. 105-107 in *Standard Edition* 14.
    London: Hogarth Press, 1957.

_____. Editor's Note to "Instincts and Their Vicissitudes,"
    by S. Freud. Pp. 111-116 in *Standard Edition* 14. London:
    Hogarth Press, 1957.

Tausk, V. "Compensation as a Means of Discounting the Motive
    of Repression." *International Journal of Psycho-Analysis*
    5 (1924) 130-140.

Trotter, W. *Instincts of the Herd in Peace and War*. London:
    T. Fisher Unwin, 1916.

Waelder, R. "The Principle of Multiple Function." *Psycho-
    analytic Quarterly* 5 (1936) 45-62.

_____. "Psychoanalysis, Scientific Method, and Philosophy."
    Journal of the American Psychoanalytic Association 10
    (1962) 617-637.

Weiss, E. "Todestrieb und Masochismus." *Imago* 21 (1935) 393-
    411.

White, R. W. *Ego and Reality in Psychoanalytic Theory*. Psy-
    chological Issues 11. New York: International Universi-
    ties Press, 1963.

Wundt, W. *Völkerpsychologie*. Vol. 2, Part II: *Mythus und
    Religion*. Leipzig, 1906.

Wyss, D. *Depth Psychology; A Critical History, Development,
    Problems, Crises*. Trans. Gerald Onn. New York: W. W.
    Norton, 1966.

Yankelovich, D., and Barrett, W. *Ego and Instinct: The Psycho-
    analytic View of Human Nature--Revised*. New York: Random
    House, 1970.

Zetzel, E. "Additional Notes Upon a Case of Obsessional Neu-
    rosis: Freud, 1909." *International Journal of Psycho-
    Analysis* 47 (1966) 123-129.

Works by Sigmund Freud

"Akute multiple Neuritis der spinalen und Hirnnerven." *Wiener
    medizinische Wochenschrift* 36/6 (1886a) 168.

With O. Rie. *Klinische Studie über die halbseitige Cerebral-
    lanmung der Kinder*. Heft III of Beiträge zur Kinderheil-
    kunde. Ed. M. Kassowitz. Vienna: Öffentliches Kinder-
    krankeninstitut, 1891a.

On Aphasia. London/New York: Imago, 1953 (1891b).

"Some Points for a Comparative Study of Organic and Hysterical
    Motor Paralyses." *SE* 1.157-172. Trans. and ed. James
    Strachey. London: Hogarth Press and the Institute of
    Psycho-Analysis, 1966 (1893c).

With J. Breuer. *Studies on Hysteria. SE* 2 (1955 [1895d]).

"Further Remarks on the Neuro-Psychoses of Defence." *SE* 3
    (1962 [1896b]) 159-185.

"The Aetiology of Hysteria." *SE* 3 (1962 [1896c]) 189-221.

The Interpretation of Dreams. SE 4 and 5 (1953 [1900a]).

The Psychopathology of Everyday Life. SE 6 (1960 [1901b]).

"On Psychotherapy." *SE* 7 (1953 [1905a]) 257-268.

Jokes and Their Relation to the Unconscious. SE 8 (1960 [1905c]).

Three Essays on the Theory of Sexuality. SE 7 (1953 [1905d])
    125-243.

"Fragment of an Analysis of a Case of Hysteria." *SE* 7 (1953
    [1905e]) 3-122.

Delusions and Dreams in Jensen's 'Gradiva.' SE 9 (1959 [1907a])
    3-95.

"Obsessive Actions and Religious Practices." *SE* 9 (1959 [1907b])
    116-127.

"The Sexual Enlightenment of Children." *SE* 9 (1959 [1907c])
    131-139.

"'Civilized' Sexual Morality and Modern Nervous Illness."
    SE 9 (1959 [1908d]) 179-204.

"Creative Writers and Day-Dreaming." *SE* 9 (1959 [1908a]) 143-
    153.

"Analysis of a Phobia in a Five-Year-Old Boy." *SE* 10 (1955
    [1909b]) 3-147.

"Notes upon a Case of Obsessional Neurosis." *SE* 10 (1955
    [1909d]) 155-318.

Leonardo da Vinci and a Memory of His Childhood. SE 11 (1957
    [1910c]) 59-137.

"The Antithetical Meaning of Primal Words." *SE* 11 (1957
    [1910e]) 155-161.

"Formulations on the Two Principles of Mental Functioning."
    SE 12 (1958 [1911b]) 215-226.

"Psycho-Analytic Notes on an Autobiographical Account of a Case of Paranoia (Demential Paranoides)." *SE* 12 (1958 [1911c]) 3-82.

"The Significance of Vowel Sequences." *SE* 12 (1958 [1911d]) 341.

"Great is Diana of the Ephesians." *SE* 12 (1958 [1911f]) 342-344.

"Postscript to the Case of Paranoia." *SE* 12 (1958 [1912a]) 80-82.

"The Dynamics of Transference." *SE* 12 (1958 [1912b]) 99-108.

"Recommendations to Physicians Practising Psycho-Analysis." *SE* 12 (1958 [1912e]) 111-120.

"A Note on the Unconscious in Psycho-Analysis." *SE* 12 (1958 [1912g]) 257-266.

Totem and Taboo. *SE* 13 (1953 [1912-1913]) 1-161.

"On Beginning the Treatment (Further Recommendations on the Technique of Psycho-Analysis, I)." *SE* 12 (1958 [1913c]) 123-144.

"The Occurrence in Dreams of Material from Fairy Tales." *SE* 12 (1958 [1913d]) 281-287.

"The Theme of the Three Caskets." *SE* 12 (1958 [1913f]) 291-301.

"The Disposition to Obsessional Neurosis." *SE* 12 (1958 [1913i]) 313-326.

"The Claims of Psycho-Analysis to Scientific Interest." *SE* 13 (1953 [1913j]) 165-190.

"Preface to J. G. Bourke's *Scatalogic Rites of all Nations.*" *SE* 12 (1958 [1913k]) 335-337.

"The Moses of Michelangelo." *SE* 13 (1953 [1914b]) 211-238.

"On Narcissism: an Introduction." *SE* 14 (1957 [1914c]) 69-102.

"On the History of the Psycho-Analytic Movement." *SE* 14 (1957 [1914d]) 3-66.

"Remembering, Repeating and Working-Through (Further Recommendations on the Technique of Psycho-Analysis, II)." *SE* 12 (1958 [1914g]) 147-156.

"Observations on Transference-Love (Further Recommendations on the Technique of Psycho-Analysis, III)." *SE* 12 (1958 [1915a]) 159-171.

"Thoughts for the Times on War and Death." *SE* 14 (1957 [1915b])
    257-300.

"Instincts and Their Vicissitudes." *SE* 14 (1957 [1915c]) 111-
    140.

"Repression." *SE* 14 (1957 [1915d]) 143-158.

"The Unconscious." *SE* 14 (1957 [1915e]) 161-215.

"A Mythological Parallel to a Visual Obsession." *SE* 14
    (1957 [1916b]) 337-338.

Introductory Lectures on Psycho-Analysis. *SE* 15 and 16
    (1961 and 1963 [1916-1917]).

"A Childhood Recollection from *Dichtung und Wahrheit*." *SE* 17
    (1955 [1917b]) 147-172.

"A Metapsychological Supplement to the Theory of Dreams."
    SE 14 (1957 [1917d]) 219-235.

"Mourning and Melancholia." *SE* 14 (1957 [1917e]) 239-258.

"Preface to Reik's Ritual: Psycho-Analytic Studies." *SE* 17
    (1955 [1919g]) 259-263.

"The Uncanny." *SE* 17 (1955 [1919h]) 219-256.

Beyond the Pleasure Principle. *SE* 18 (1955 [1920g]) 7-64.

Group Psychology and the Analysis of the Ego. *SE* 18 (1955
    [1921c]) 69-143.

"Two Encyclopaedia Articles." *SE* 18 (1955 [1923a]) 235-259.

The Ego and the Id. *SE* 19 (1961 [1923b]) 3-66.

"The Infantile Genital Organization." *SE* 19 (1961 [1923e])
    141-145.

"Neurosis and Psychosis." *SE* 19 (1961 [1924b]) 149-153.

"The Economic Problem of Masochism." *SE* 19 (1961 [1924c])
    157-170.

"The Dissolution of the Oedipus Complex." *SE* 19 (1961 [1924d])
    173-179.

"The Loss of Reality in Neurosis and Psychosis." *SE* 19 (1961
    [1924e]) 183-187.

"A Note Upon the 'Mystic Writing-Pad.'" *SE* 19 (1961 [1925a])
    227-232.

An Autobiographical Study. *SE* 20 (1959 [1925d]) 3-74.

"Negation." *SE* 19 (1961 [1925h]) 235-239.

Inhibitions, Symptoms and Anxiety. *SE* 20 (1959 [1926d]) 77-174.

An Article in the Encyclopaedia Britannica (published as "Psycho-Analysis: Freudian School"). *SE* 20 (1959 [1926f]) 261-270.

The Future of an Illusion. *SE* 21 (1961 [1927c]) 3-56.

"Humor." *SE* 21 (1961 [1927d]) 159-166.

"Fetishism," *SE* 21 (1961 [1927e]) 149-157.

Civilization and its Discontents. *SE* 21 (1961 [1930a]) 59-145.

New Introductory Lectures on Psycho-Analysis. *SE* 22 (1964 [1933a]) 3-182.

Why War? *SE* 22 (1964 [1933b]) 197-215.

"A Disturbance of Memory on the Acropolis." *SE* 22 (1964 [1936a]) 239-248.

"Analysis Terminable and Interminable." *SE* 23 (1964 [1937c]) 211-253.

"Constructions in Analysis." *SE* 23 (1964 [1937d]) 257-269.

Moses and Monotheism. *SE* 23 (1964 [1939a]) 3-137.

An Outline of Psycho-Analysis. *SE* 23 (1964 [1940a] 141-207.

"Medusa's Head." *SE* 18 (1955 [1940c]) 273-274.

"Splitting of the Ego in the Process of Defence." *SE* 23 (1964 [1940e]) 273-278.

The Origins of Psycho-Analysis (partly including "A Project for a Scientific Psychology"). *SE* 1 (1966 [1950a]) 175-342

Collected Papers. 5 vols. London: Basic Books, 1959.

Gesammelte Schriften. 12 vols. Vienna: International Psychoanalytic Press, 1924-1934.

Gesammelte Werke. 18 vols. London: Imago Publishing, 1940-1968.

The Origins of Psycho-Analysis, Letters to Wilhelm Fliess, Drafts and Notes: 1887-1902. Ed. Marie Bonaparte, Anna Freud, Ernst Kris; trans. Eric Mosbacher and James Strachey. New York: Basic Books, 1954.

Psycho-Analysis and Faith. The Letters of Sigmund Freud and Oskar Pfister. London/New York: Hogarth Press, 1963.

The Freud/Jung Letters: The Correspondence Between Sigmund Freud and C. G. Jung. Ed. W. McGuire; trans. R. Manheim and R.F.C. Hull. Princeton: Princeton University, 1974.

INDEX